OUTSIDE THE RAILS

A RAIL ROUTE GUIDE FROM CHICAGO TO SOUTH BEND AIRPORT, IN

For use on the Northern Indiana Commuter Transportation District's South Shore Line Service

PUBLISHED JULY 1, 2017

Material in this reference manual was accurate to the best of our knowledge at the time of publication listed above. Note that over the years, trackside attractions may come and go. When there are significant changes a new edition may be released.

By Robert T. Tabern & Kandace M. Tabern
with an Introduction by John Kelly

Cover Photo by Russell John Sekeet

ROUTE GUIDE SYMBOLS

📷	Site Visible from Train	〰️	River Crossing
	Historical Information		Agricultural Information
△	Geology or Geography		Animal Sighting Possible
⊗	Railroad Information	☒	Amtrak® Train Station

ISBN 978-1-365-87651-6

Outside the Rails is ©2017   Robert & Kandace Tabern, All Rights Reserved

1

WELCOME ABOARD

Dear traveler,

Welcome aboard and thanks for riding the South Shore Line between Chicago's Millennium Station and South Bend Airport with the APRHF Rail Rangers!

In July 2017, the American Passenger Rail Heritage Foundation (APRHF) reached a unique partnership agreement with the Northern Indiana Commuter Transportation District (NICTD). This deal enhances the experience of passengers on the train through Illinois and Indiana, with the creation of this rail route guidebook and having APRHF Rail Rangers' Interpretive Guides provide on-board programs on select departures. Guides explain what passengers are seeing out their window, in addition to telling brief stories about the people, places, and history of the region.

We hope you will enjoy your train trip and that you will learn a lot of interesting stories from your purchase of this route guidebook. To find out when APRHF Rail Rangers will be presenting live educational programs on future train trips between Chicago and South Bend, you can check out our websites, www.railrangers.org, or www.southshoreline.org.

Thanks,
Robert Tabern, Rail Rangers Executive Director / APRHF Vice-President
Bob Cox, La Plata Coordinator / APRHF President
Kandace Tabern, Rail Rangers Chicago Coordinator
Amy Cox, Rail Rangers Assistant La Plata Coordinator

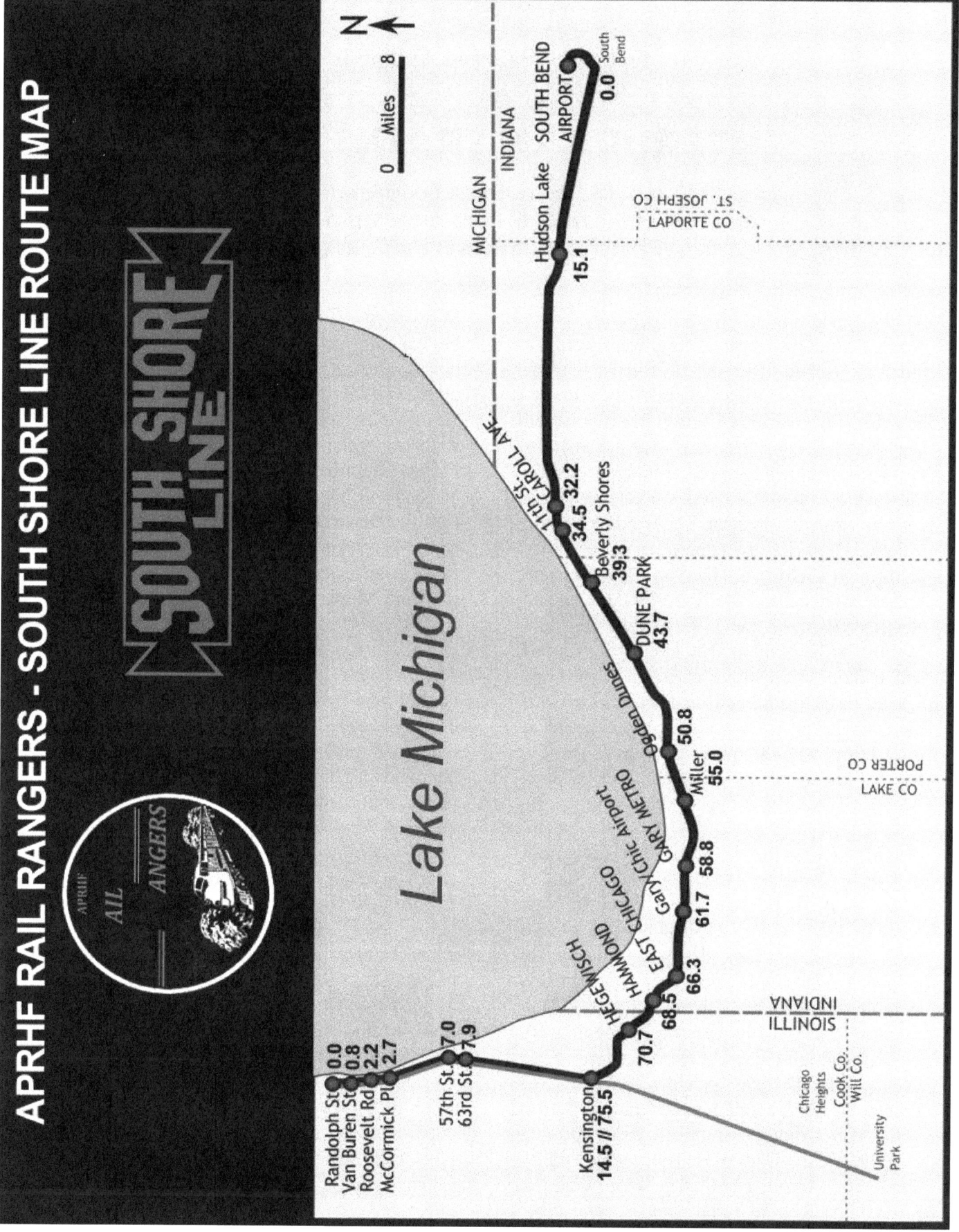

An Introduction by Railroad Author John Kelly

INTERURBAN TRAINS TO CHICAGO

John Kelly, a published author of numerous railroad books, and avid supporter of the APRHF Rail Rangers, provides a brief overview of interurban trains in the Chicagoland area.

At the beginning of the 20th Century, most people did not own a car and highways were not much more than dirt roads. The most popular means of transportation were actually walking, horse-drawn carriage, and steam-powered heavyweight trains. That was also the dawn of the interurban (high-speed, intercity electric railways operating on overhead catenary) that evolved from the streetcar. The word interurban is derived from Latin for "between cities" and is credited to Charles L. Henry, an Indiana state senator who coined the term after seeing the electric railway at the 1893 Chicago World's Columbian Exposition. The interurbans' speed and handiness operating at frequent intervals carried passengers, mail, express, and general merchandise from the city to the country. It brought farmers and out-of-town folks into the city for a day of shopping and helped open America's suburbs to new development.

One of the most famous business tycoons from the Interurban Era was Chicago's Samuel Insull. Born in London, Insull came to New York in 1881, at age 21, and became private secretary to inventor Thomas Edison. He helped Edison build electric power stations throughout the United States, and with Edison founded the General Electric Company. By 1892, Insull left General Electric and moved to Chicago to become president of Chicago Edison. In 1907, Insull merged Chicago Edison with rival Commonwealth Electric, forming Commonwealth Edison. He later merged utility companies forming Middle West Utilities, providing power to Illinois and several other Midwestern states. Meanwhile, Insull had been buying substantial stock in many railroads, mostly electric interurban streetcar lines. The most well-known of Insull's interurban lines was the Chicago North Shore and Milwaukee Railroad, often referred to as "America's Fastest Interurban". In 1916, Insull acquired the bankrupt Chicago & Milwaukee Electric Railway, renamed it the Chicago North Shore and Milwaukee, and converted it into a first-class electric interurban railway. The line ran from Milwaukee to Evanston, Illinois, and by 1919, North Shore trains were operating into the Chicago Loop over the existing Northwestern Elevated Railroad. Passengers could travel between Chicago and Milwaukee on the luxury *Badger Limited*, complete with diner and parlor-observation cars. The train operated on a 2 hour and 15 minute schedule on newly built roadbed between the two cities. On February 15, 1922, the North Shore introduced its new *Eastern Limited*, operating over the South Side Elevated Railroad to a terminal at 63rd and Dorchester on Chicago's South Side, with hourly service to Milwaukee and connections to eastern railroads. North Shore passengers taking the *Twentieth Century Limited* transferred directly at La Salle Street Station, and passengers for the *Broadway Limited* could walk from the Wells & Quincy elevated station to Chicago Union Station. In 1925, the North Shore was operating 160 trains daily between Milwaukee and Chicago, and passenger traffic counts increased to 16-million riders annually.

Photograph of Samuel Insull
(Public domain image)

A North Shore Line train in the 1920's
(Courtesy: Waukegan News Sun)

By 1924, the railroad's Shore Line Route between Chicago and Waukegan was becoming more congested due to urban sprawl in the shoreline communities, speed restrictions, and exhibiting grade curvature. North Shore management believed future passenger growth would require expansion from two tracks to a four-track route, a project that would be costly as land and building values continued to increase along Lake Michigan's shoreline. As an alternative plan, the railroad decided to build a new, direct cutoff through the Skokie Valley on land owned by an Insull business (Public Service Company of Northern Illinois) for high-speed transmission lines. The 23-mile Skokie Valley Route was built on this right-of-way west of Lake Bluff, eventually connecting to the Howard Street "L" at Evanston, and into Chicago. It was three miles shorter than the old Shore Line Route and allowed express train operations, plus increased suburban ridership into Chicago. Construction of the new route began April 4, 1924, and was completed June 5, 1926, at a cost of ten million dollars. Opening of the Skokie Valley Route was observed with much fanfare and hope for the future, including faster Chicago-Milwaukee trains. The Cincinnati Car Company built 20 steel interurban cars and three dining cars for the new service. Gross operating revenue for 1926 increased to $7.6 million and ridership boomed to an all-time high of 19.5 million passengers, with continued growth in 1928. Of course, it didn't last; the 1929 stock market crash followed by the 1930's Great Depression began three decades of decline for the North Shore. In 1932, the mighty Insull Empire went bust, as thousands of small investors were wiped out. Insull was indicated for unfair business practices and forced to resign. He fled to Europe to avoid prosecution, but was returned to the United States for trial in 1934. Insull was found not guilty and was vindicated of all charges. He returned to Europe and on July 16, 1938, died of a heart attack in a Paris Metro station.

A 1927 timetable for the new Skokie Valley Line
(Public domain image)

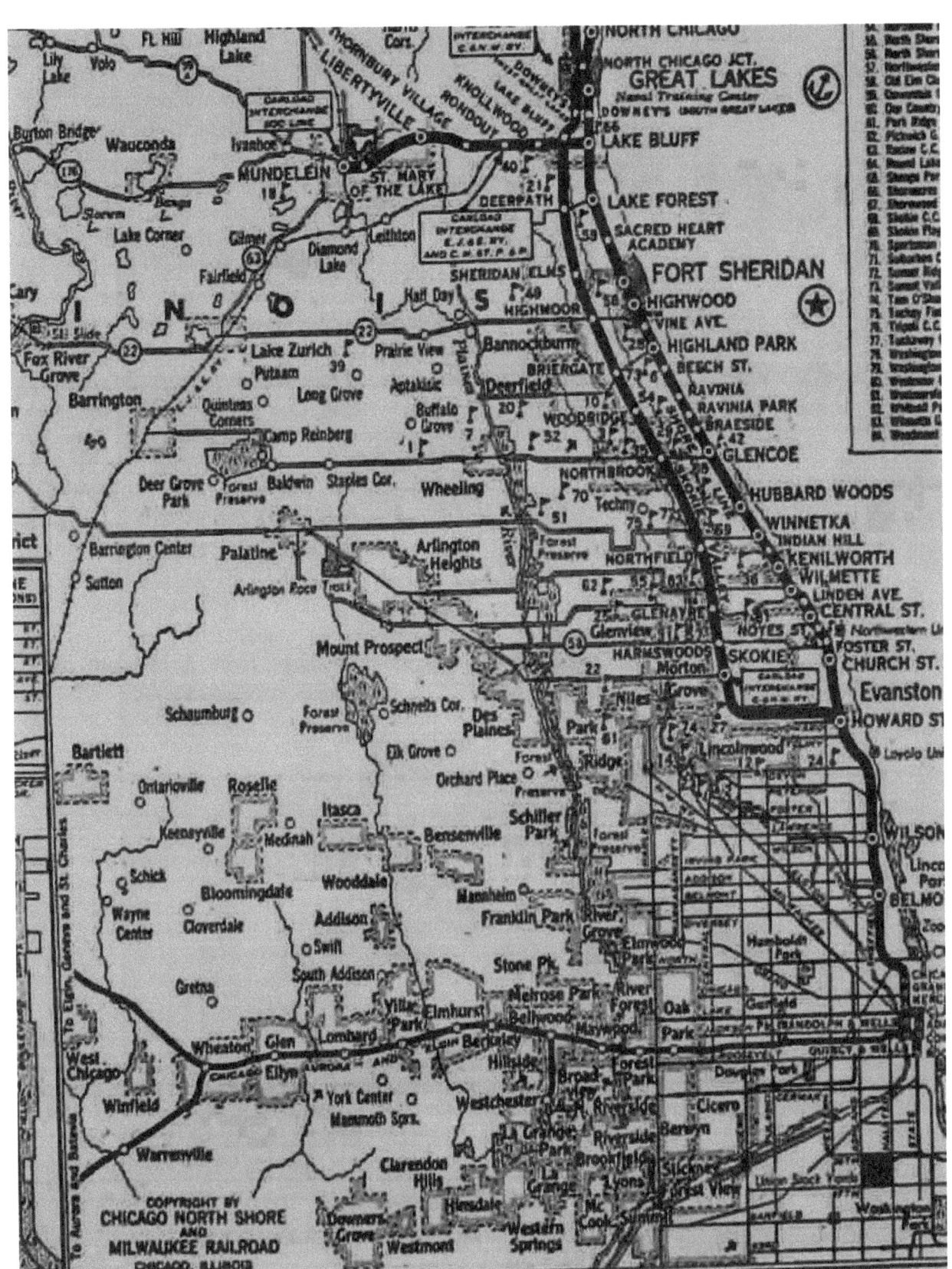

A North Shore Line map from the 1930's
(Public domain image)

*A postcard of the North Shore Line's Electroliner
(Public domain image)*

The North Shore Line continued on with new leadership and entered the streamlined era in 1941 with a modern set of interurban trains called Electroliners for Chicago-Milwaukee service. The four-section articulated trains built by the St. Louis Car Company carried 120 passengers in soundproof cabs and both smoking and non-smoking coach seating. An additional car provided coach seating for 30 passengers, plus a smoking-coach section for ten. The Tavern-Lounge car seated 26, serving light meals and beverages. Tavern-Lounge décor was a coal-brown and gold scheme with colorful animal characters on the upper wall. Electroliner exterior colors were blue-green trimmed in salmon-red striping with lettering and lightning bolt logo. After inaugural runs the Electroliners began revenue service February 9, 1941, with five roundtrips daily between Chicago and Milwaukee. During their first year in operation, 395,318 passengers rode the Electroliners and in 1942 that figure nearly doubled to 641,096. Eventually, the newly built Chicago expressways, combined with the automobile's popularity, forced the North Shore into abandonment. Finally, on January 21, 1963, the trolley poles were hooked down for the last time and the Chicago North Shore and Milwaukee Railroad era was over.

*North Shore Line equipment preserved today at the Illinois Railroad Museum in Union, IL
(Courtesy: Illinois Railroad Museum)*

*Chicago Aurora and Elgin Railroad Map
(Public domain image)*

Another Insull-owned interurban line was the Chicago Aurora and Elgin Railroad, originally founded in 1899 as the Aurora Wheaton and Chicago Railroad. By 1903, the company built an electric rail line using 600-volt third rail from 52nd Avenue in Chicago to Aurora, with branch lines to Wheaton, Batavia, and Elgin, Illinois. In 1909, the line was extended to Geneva and St. Charles, Illinois. At that time, access to Downtown Chicago was via the Metropolitan Westside Elevated Railway-Garfield Park Branch elevated lines. Following World War I, the railroad was re-organized as the Chicago Aurora and Elgin Railroad on July 1, 1922. Samuel Insull's Middle West Utilities gained control of the railroad in 1926, and remained under Insull's control until bankruptcy in 1932. The CA&E recovered from bankruptcy in 1946 and continued to be an important commuter line. The railroad carried 30,000 riders a day over 52 miles of track from the western suburbs into Chicago's Wells Street Terminal. Most of the route was electrified third rail with short sections of overhead trolley at the west end of the line, so CA&E cars were equipped with both third rail shoes and trolley poles. In 1953, the City of Chicago approved building the Congress Street Expressway (now called the Eisenhower) over the Metropolitan Elevated tracks, which the railroad used for access to downtown. With the expressway completed and the Metropolitan Elevated tracks demolished, CA&E passengers could only ride to Forest Park, where they had to make an across-platform transfer to Chicago Transit Authority trains. CA&E riders had lost their one-seat ride into Downtown Chicago. Nicknamed the "Sunset Lines" because it carried commuters straight west into the sunset from Chicago's Wells Street Terminal to the western suburbs, the Chicago Aurora and Elgin Railroad continued to operate with declining ridership until July 3, 1957, when passenger service ended. Freight traffic continued until 1959 and total abandonment of the line was approved in 1961.

A Chicago Aurora and Elgin ticket
(Public domain image)

A restored Chicago Aurora and Elgin car at the Illinois Railroad Museum in Union, IL
(Courtesy: Illinois Railroad Museum)

*Historical photo of a Chicago Lake Shore and South Bend Railroad car
(Courtesy: Illinois Railroad Museum)*

The earliest predecessor to Insull's South Shore Lines was the Chicago & Indiana Air Line Railway, incorporated December 2, 1901, as a streetcar operation between Indiana Harbor and East Chicago. By 1908, it was known as the Chicago Lake Shore and South Bend Railroad, extending across Northwest Indiana to South Bend (90 miles). Being a smart investor, Insull recognized the potential of hauling inbould coal to the generating stations and Indiana steel mills, and in 1925 he purchased the railroad, renaming it the Chicago South Shore and South Bend. Insull began a modernization program in 1925, building new bridges, passenger stations, and passenger cars. In addition, the railroad updated from wood interurban cars running on 6,600-volts A.C. to modern steel cars operating on 1,500-volts D.C., with substations built by Insull-controlled Northern Indiana Public Service Company. On August 29, 1926, South Shore trains began operating over Illinois Central's electrified route from Kensington, Illinois to Randolph Street in Downtown Chicago. Insull's improvements paid off, as ridership increased from 60,000 in 1926 to 140,000 in 1927. By 1928, the South Shore was operating with profitability, including on-line freight businesses. World War II ridership helped increase revenue, but like other interurban lines the big orange and maroon cars were doomed by the post-World War II sprawling suburbs and affordable automobiles. The South Shore responded with fare increases and service cuts, but reduction led to further ridership losses. In 1976, the South Shore petitioned the federal government for discontinuance of passenger service, and in 1977, the State of Indiana created the Northern Indiana Commuter Transportation District (NICTD) to restore service on the South Shore route. Today, the regional-managed NICTD Shore Shore Line between South Bend and Chicago operates fast, reliable, and modern electric trains on the former Chicago South Shore and South Bend route into Downtown Chicago's Millennium Station (formerly Randolph Street Station).

A South Shore Line train passes through Downtown Chicago on the Illinois Central
(Public domain image)

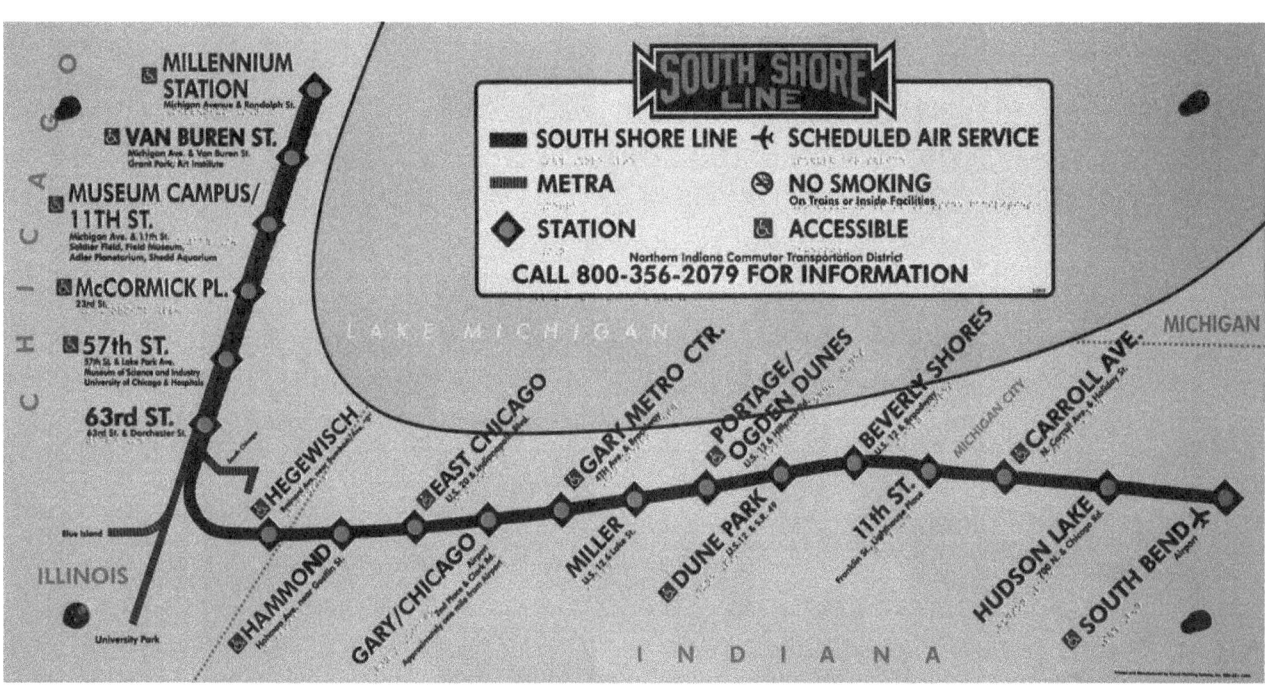

Map of the South Shore Line
(Courtesy: Northern Indiana Commuter Transportation District)

Street running on the South Shore Line in Michigan City, Indiana
(Public domain image)

Bi-level cars, built in 2009, operate on some of the South Shore Line runs
(Courtesy: Monon Railroad Historical-Technical Society)

Besides the North Shore Line, the CA&E, and the South Shore, two other small interurban lines also served Chicago. The Chicago and Southern Traction Company, later named Chicago and Interurban Traction, ran a 54-mile line from the 63rd and Halsted "L" Station in Chicago to Kankakee, Illinois. The Kankakee Line, as it was called, ended service in 1927.

The other Chicago interurban was the Chicago and Joliet Electric, operating from Joliet, Illinois, to Archer and Cicero Avenues in Chicago, near what is today Midway Airport. The railroad lasted until 1933 when it went out of business.

The Interurban Era had developed primarily after World War I, but its decline began shortly after. By the mid-1930's, most interurban lines were out of business; a few continued to operate in large American cities but most were gone by 1950. However, the interurbans' brief life cycle changed America forever, bridging the gap from horse and buggy to private automobiles, interstate highways, commuter trains, and suburbia.

About John Kelly

John Kelly grew up in Eau Claire, Wisconsin, where his father's best friend was an engineer on the Chicago & North Western. John has been collecting railroad photos, timetables and dining car menus for 30 years and has a large collection. In addition, he has written on railroad history for Trains Magazine, Trains.com, Vintage Rails, Passenger Train Journal, and has authored more than a dozen other photographic books on vintage trains. John lives in Madison, Wisconsin with his partner Linda. He is enjoying retirement after working as a computer technician for the Wisconsin Technical College system. If you rode the *Empire Builder* between Chicago and Winona, Minnesota anytime between 2007 and 2010, you may recognize John as one of the Trails & Rails docents who presented on-board educational programs to passengers. He also served as an Interpretive Guide for the APRHF-sponsored Trails & Rails program that took place on the *Southwest Chief* between 2013 and 2015. While retired from his Interpretive Guide role, John remains a strong supporter of the Rail Rangers program and its new mission on the South Shore Line.

CHICAGO
(Population 2,722,389; Elevation: 594 feet)

*Various images of Chicago landmarks
(Public domain images)*

This route guide begins at Chicago, Illinois, the third largest city in the United States. Currently, Chicago has a population of 2.7 million people; the entire metropolitan area has 9.5 million.

The first European explorers to set foot on the site destined to become Chicago were Louis Joliet and Father Jacques Marquette. The two explorers were commissioned by the French government in 1673. Father Marquette returned to the area one year later to establish an Indian mission. Chicago's first actual permanent settler, Jean Baptiste Point DuSable, came to the area around 1780. He traded furs with the Indians on the north bank of the Chicago River, where he lived with his wife, Catherine, until 1796. He and his wife then left with their children and moved to Peoria, Illinois.

In 1803, the U.S. Army built Fort Dearborn; it was located along the banks of the Chicago River, near where Michigan Avenue crosses it today. During the War of 1812, this fort and most of the small surrounding community were destroyed in a surprise attack by a group of Potawatomi Indians. A second fort was rebuilt a few years later. By 1833, the Town of Chicago was organized with a population of around 200. Chicago became incorporated as a city in 1837.

*Site of Fort Dearborn is marked in downtown
(Photo by Robert Tabern)*

During the mid-1800's, Chicago was one of the fastest growing cities in the world; this was due to its prime location for shipping goods. In 1848, the first railroad began running through Chicago. This year also marked the opening of the Illinois & Michigan Canal, which provided a direct waterway link between the Great Lakes and the Mississippi River. Chicago became a real leader in the cattle, hog, lumber, and wheat industries. The years leading up to the Civil War brought as many as 100,000 immigrants per year arriving in Chicago seeking work.

In 1860, Chicago gained attention for hosting the Republican National Convention, which nominated Illinois' own Abraham Lincoln as a presidential candidate. One year later, during Lincoln's first term, the Civil War began. Post-war Chicago was unstoppable; the population grew, grain shipments doubled, and merchants prospered.

In October 1871, the Great Chicago Fire broke out, destroying an area four miles long and one mile wide; this was a large section of the city.

*An illustration of the Great Chicago Fire
(Public domain image)*

After the fire, a greater Chicago emerged. Internationally acclaimed architects flocked to the city for its reconstruction. Within a few years, Chicago was resurrected, including the building of the world's first skyscraper in 1885. Chicago was on the international stage when it was chosen to host the 1893 World Columbian Exposition for millions of visitors.

*The World's Columbian Exposition of 1893
(Public domain image)*

Today, Chicago is a dynamic and culturally diverse city. It is an international center for business and leisure travel, due in part to the city's transportation accessibility, a thriving business community, and world-class hotels, restaurants, shopping, and attractions.

COOK COUNTY, ILLINOIS

The City of Chicago, which our South Shore Line train will travel through for about 20.8 miles before reaching the Illinois-Indiana State Line, is located in Cook County, Illinois. This is the only Illinois county we pass through.

Cook County has 5.2 million residents, making it the second most populous county in the United States (after Los Angeles County, CA). More than 40% of Illinois' residents call this county home. The U.S. Census Bureau reports Cook County has actually more residents than 29 individual U.S. states, and the combined population of the seven smallest states.

Cook County was created out of Putnam County on January 15, 1831, by an act of the Illinois General Assembly. It was the 54th county established in Illinois, and was named after Daniel Cook. Cook was one of the youngest statesmen in Illinois history, serving as the second U.S. Representative from Illinois, and also as the state's first Attorney General. In 1839, DuPage County was carved out of Cook County. Today, Cook County is the fifth largest employer in Chicago.

CHICAGO MILLENNIUM STATION
(Milepost 0.0) (41.8843° N, 87.6229° W)

Interior of Millennium Station, as seen today
(Public domain image)

The history of what is now called Millennium Station dates back to the year 1856. Illinois Central Railroad built an above-ground train station called Great Central Station (also known as Great Central Depot) at the site of today's Millennium Station – at Michigan Avenue and Randolph Street. When completed, it became the largest building in Downtown Chicago. It was damaged in the Great Chicago Fire of 1871, but remained in operation.

An 1856 illustration of Great Central Station
(Public domain image)

Some twenty years, Chicago's Great Central Station became inadequate to handle all of the Illinois Central's passenger train traffic. In anticipation of the 1893 World Columbian Exposition, the railroad decided to build a new much larger station about two miles south, near Michigan Avenue and Roosevelt Road. The new Central Station became the main terminal for intercity passenger trains. The station was designed with run-through tracks that enabled some trains to continue north to the old Great Central Station, which was re-named Randolph Street Station to avoid any confusion with the new terminal.

Randolph Street Station, as seen in 1895
(Public domain image)

Between 1893 and 1926, Randolph Street Station still received many trains, but was of secondary importance to Central Station. It mainly served Illinois Central suburban trains operating as far south as Richton Park. Some improvements were added during this time period, like the 1921 pedestrian tunnel linking the station to the corner of Randolph Street and Michigan Avenue.

Around the same time, people who lived and worked around Downtown Chicago began to complain to city officials about the air pollution being generated by idling steam trains at Randolph and other stations. This led to city ordinances which made the Illinois Central electrify its commuter rail lines by 1926.

Through a trackage-rights agreement with the Illinois Central, Chicago South Shore and South Bend interurban electric trains began operating out of Randolph Street Station in 1926 as well. The deal not only included shared use of stations, but also gave South Shore Line trains the right to operate over the first 14.5 miles of the Illinois Central main line to a point known as Kensington. This is the same route our South Shore Line train to South Bend will operate on today. New platforms were installed on the east end of Randolph Street Station for these trains.

By the 1930's, vacant land for new buildings was at a premium in Downtown Chicago. The Illinois Central decided to construct a new five-track facility below ground level for its suburban trains. The new Randolph Station simplified construction of office buildings above the tracks by using something known as "air rights". The configuration of the station changed again when the Prudential Building was constructed in the early 1950's. A new waiting room and ticket office were built one floor below street level and one floor above track level. A total of 11 tracks came into this redesigned station – six were used by IC trains and five by the South Shore. Many commuters did not like the changes and felt the windowless station provided a dark, cave-like environment, especially compared to other grand stations.

Randolph Street Station, as seen in 1965 (Public domain image)

Randolph Street Station existed in a state of perpetual construction from the mid-1980's until 2005. If you took the South Shore during this period, you will likely remember exposed steel girders covered in flame retardant, unpainted plywood walls, bare concrete floors, and dim utility lights. Water issues with the roof meant the entire structure had to be rebuilt and this was not an easy process due to how the Prudential Center was constructed.

Ownership of Randolph Street Station and the railroad also changed hands during this period, leading to even more construction delays. The famed Illinois Central merged with the Gulf, Mobile, and Ohio Railroad in 1972 to form the Illinois Central Gulf Railroad. Over the next few years, the company became interested in its more lucrative freight traffic, desperately wanting out of running a commuter operation between Chicago and its southern suburbs. By May 1987, Metra bought the former Illinois Central electrified commuter tracks and its stations. Trackage agreements were kept in place to allow South Shore trains to operate on the line from Randolph Station to Kensington.

When construction was completed in 2006, Randolph was re-named as Millennium Station; it coincides with the nearby park. The current station was designed by the award-winning architectural firm of Skidmore, Owings & Merrill. Their employees have completed over 10,000 projects around the United States and in more than 50 other countries around the world. Their work includes the Burj Khalifa, the tallest man-made structure ever built, and One World Trade Center, better known as the new Freedom Tower in Lower Manhattan, New York City. In the past decade, numerous restaurants and shops have opened in the new Millennium Station, making it a lot more pleasant place to wait for your outbound train than in years past. Some have suggested that future improvements could include a direct link to Millennium Park or a more easily identifiable entrance.

*The boarding area for South Shore Line trains
(Public domain image)*

MILLENNIUM PARK
(Milepost 0.1) (41.8826° N, 87.6229° W)

The first three blocks of our trip out of Millennium Station is through an underground tunnel; above us lies Millennium Park. A new report that came out in April 2017 indicates that Millennium Park is the top tourist attraction both in Chicago and the entire Midwestern United States (Navy Pier used to hold this title). The free park east of the Loop hosted 12.9 million visitors in the second half of 2016 alone, according to Chicago's Department of Cultural Affairs and Special Events. Since our train is traveling through a tunnel underneath the park, we won't be able to see any of it – however it's worth a stop on your next visit.

Planning of the park began in October 1997, with actual construction beginning one year later. Millennium Park was opened in a ceremony on July 16, 2004, four years behind schedule. The three-day opening celebrations were attended by some 300,000 people and included an inaugural concert by the Grant Park Orchestra and Chorus. The park has received awards for its accessibility and green design. Millennium Park has free admission, and features the Jay Pritzker Pavilion, *Cloud Gate*, the *Crown Fountain*, the Lurie Garden, and various other attractions. The park is connected by the BP Pedestrian Bridge and the Nichols Bridgeway to other parts of Grant Park. Because the park sits atop a parking garage and Millennium Station, it is considered the world's largest rooftop garden.

*Cloud Gate in Millennium Park
(Public domain image)*

One of the most popular features of Millennium Park is a sculpture known as *Cloud Gate*; it is pictured above. Constructed between 2004 and 2006, it has been nicknamed "The Bean" because of its shape. Made up of 168 stainless steel plates welded together, its highly polished exterior has no visible seams. It measures 33x66x42 feet and weighs around 100 tons. It was designed by Indian-born British artist Anish Kapoor, who said he was inspired by liquid mercury. Since the sculpture's surface reflects the skyline and can distort what people look like, it has become a popular place for tourists to stop and snap a picture.

Between May and October, you may want to check out *Crown Fountain*, which is located just south of *Cloud Gate* in Millennium Park. The fountain is composed of a black granite reflecting pool and a pair of 50 feet high glass brick towers. The towers use LEDs to display digital videos of different people's faces. At some point the mouth on the face begins to pucker and water is shot out at unsuspecting tourists.

Rail Rangers Guides enjoy Cloud Gate
(Photo by Robert Tabern)

THE ART INSTITUTE OF CHICAGO
(Milepost 0.6) (41.8795° N, 87.6229° W)

Our train will emerge into daylight after crossing underneath Monroe Street (Milepost 0.5). For the next few miles, we travel below street level in a rail trench through the south side of Downtown Chicago. One of the most notable trackside buildings is the Art Institute of Chicago, visible just after Monroe Street.

The Art Institute of Chicago
(Public domain image)

The original Art Institute of Chicago building is west of the tracks; it was completed in 1893 for the World's Columbian Exposition. When the art museum campus was expanded to include a new building east of the Illinois Central tracks in the 1920's, a walkway was built that our train will pass underneath. Train passengers mainly see the newer building. Today, the Art Institute of Chicago is recognized as one of the oldest and largest art museums in the United States. Its permanent collection features nearly 300,000 works of art, with approximately 1.5 million visitors passing through the doors every year. Some of the famous paintings that you can see include Edward Hopper's *Nighthawks* and Pablo Picasso's *The Old Guitarist*.

Kids enjoy playing in the Crown Fountain
(Public domain image)

If you're visiting Millennium Park in the winter instead, make sure you stop by the popular McCormick Tribune Plaza & Ice Rink. Even if you don't strap on skates yourself, it's a fun place to enjoy a hot chocolate and watch others skate around the outdoor rink.

VAN BUREN STREET STATION
(Milepost 0.8) (41.8770° N, 87.6229° W)

South Shore passengers at Van Buren Street
(Public domain image)

Interior of the Van Buren Street Station
(Public domain image)

Van Buren Street is the first intermediate station stop for eastbound South Shore Line trains; it is located less than one mile south of Randolph Street. Passenger stations from here to Kensington are "receive only", meaning passengers may only board South Shore trains for destinations in Indiana. No passengers may de-train. Per the trackage rights agreement, passengers who want to travel locally must use Metra's service. This prevents the South Shore from potentially "competing" against Metra, which owns and operates the tracks.

Illinois Central opened the Van Buren Street station in 1896 to serve the south side of Downtown Chicago. This stop was primarily for suburban trains since most intercity trains terminated to the south at Roosevelt Road. The station also provided a more direct link than Randolph Street to those who were looking to transfer to intercity trains operated by other railroads, such as Union Station. The interior of the station was restored to its historic appearance and is worth a visit. Van Buren Street remains the oldest station still in operation on both the South Shore Line and Metra's Electric District lines.

GRANT PARK
(Milepost 1.0) (41.8770° N, 87.6229° W)

Chicago's Grant Park
(Public domain image)

South of Van Buren Street, we remain in the railroad trench, while Grant Park appears above us on both sides of the train. Originally known as Lake Park, and dating from the city's founding, it was renamed in 1901 to honor Ulysses S. Grant. The 319-acre park contains various performance venues, gardens, art work, sporting, and harbor facilities. Not visible because of being in the trench, the train passes about one block away from the popular Buckingham Fountain, one of the largest fountains in the world.

The back side of this statue can be seen from the train in Grant Park, just south of Van Buren Station

Tucked away in a lonely corner of Grant Park is one of the city's greatest war memorials. Gen. John A. Logan is depicted on horseback rallying his troops during the Civil War. Logan was born in Murphysboro, Illinois in 1826. He fought at Bull Run as an unattached volunteer in a Michigan regiment, and then entered the Union Army as Colonel of an Illinois Volunteer Infantry Regiment, which he organized. He was known by his soldiers with the nickname "Black John" because of his black eyes and hair and swarthy complexion, and was regarded as one of the most able officers to enter the army from civilian life. Besides the First Battle of Bull Run, Logan was also present for the Battle of Fort Donelson, the Second Battle of Corinth, the Vicksburg Campaign, and Battle of Atlanta Logan was also a congressman and a senator.

This statue by Augustus Saint-Guadens and Alexander Phimister is given a prominent place atop a small artificial knoll near 9th Street. Unfortunately, it elevates the statue out of pedestrian sight lines and it ends up obscured behind trees most of the year. However, it is visible from the train line; look to west about two blocks south of Van Buren Street station.

It is a curious fact that Chicago's two most prominent lakefront parks host a contradiction: there is a statue of Ulysses S. Grant in Lincoln Park (on the city's north side) and a statue of President Abraham Lincoln here in Grant Park. No alderman, to our knowledge, has ever yet suggested that the statues of Grant and Lincoln be switched for the sake of consistency. But we still wouldn't put it past them!

Buckingham Fountain in Grant Park
(Public domain image)

MUSEUM CAMPUS / 11TH STREET
(Milepost 1.4) (41.8770° N, 87.6229° W)

[X] Museum Campus/11th Street is the second intermediate station stop for eastbound South Shore Line trains. This station opened in 2009, replacing the rickety and run-down commuter platforms that were still left over from Illinois Central's Central Station.

Just west of the current station once stood the pride and joy of the Illinois Central – Central Station. The nine-story building featured a 13-story clock tower and housed the general offices of the railroad. It boasted the largest train shed in the world when it opened in 1893, measuring 140 by 610 feet.

Like all passenger railroads across the United States, the Illinois Central saw a dramatic drop in demand during the 1950's as more people drove and flew. By 1971, Amtrak took over all of the Illinois Central's long-distance passenger service. To make connections easier, Amtrak consolidated all of it railroad operations into Chicago's Union Station. No longer serving a purpose, most of Central Station was torn down in 1974. Even though they were in rather poor shape, the commuter platforms survived another three decades until the current Museum Campus/11th Street station opened.

Historical photo of Central Station
(Public domain image)

The station here provides an easy walk over to the Field Museum, Shedd Aquarium, and Adler Planetarium for travelers.

View of the current Metra/South Shore station
(Public domain image)

THE FIELD MUSEUM
(Milepost 1.5) (41.8660° N, 87.6204° W)

*Chicago's Field Museum
(Public domain image)*

📷 Even though we are still below street level when departing Museum Campus/11th Street, the train will past just a block or so west of the Field Museum of Natural History. The museum and its collections originate from the 1893 World's Columbian Exposition and the various artifacts displayed at the fair. The museum was named after its first major benefactor, Marshall Field, founder of the famous department store. Today, around two million people visit every year, enjoying exhibits which range from the earliest fossils to past and current cultures from around the world. One of the "must see" exhibits includes Sue, the most complete and best-preserved Tyrannosaurus rex fossil.

*"Sue" at Chicago's Field Museum
(Public domain image)*

SOLDIER FIELD
(Milepost 1.8) (41.8660° N, 87.6204° W)

📷 South of the Field Museum, but also on the east side of the tracks, stands Soldier Field – home of the Chicago Bears.

*Soldier Field in Chicago
(Public domain image)*

Soldier Field was designed in 1919 and opened on October 9, 1924, as Municipal Grant Park Stadium. The name was changed to Soldier Field on November 11, 1925, as a memorial to U.S. soldiers who had died in combat. Its formal dedication as Soldier Field came the following year during the 29th annual playing of the Army-Navy Game. Soldier Field was used as a site for many sporting events and exhibitions over the years.

The Chicago Bears began playing at Soldier Field in September 1971. They previously played at Wrigley Field, best known as the home of the Chicago Cubs baseball team. The Bears were forced to move to a larger venue due to post-AFL-NFL merger policies requiring stadiums to seat 50,000+ spectators.

A renovation in 2003 that added modern grandstands extending well above the original Neoclassical columns caused Soldier Field to get de-listed as a National Historic Landmark.

18TH STREET YARD
(Milepost 2.0) (41.8600° N, 87.6186° W)

Metra Electric trains in the 18th Street Yard (Public domain image)

South of Soldier Field, our train will pass through Metra's 18th Street Yard. This facility was constructed by the Illinois Central Railroad in the 1920's, and inherited by Metra when it took over commuter train operations in 1987.

Most Metra commuter trains on this line are kept in train yards located in the south suburbs during the overnight hours. This makes sense since most commuters begin their day in the suburbs and commute into Downtown Chicago as part of the morning rush hour. However, what happens to these trains during the work day? There are not enough empty tracks at Randolph Street Station for trains to just sit there for eight hours waiting for the evening commute to roll around. Likewise, since there is going to be a huge demand for trains to leave Downtown Chicago around 5:00 p.m., it would not make sense to send all trains back to the south suburban yards following the morning rush. That is where the 18th Street Yard comes into play. Many trains are brought here for maintenance and other service work during the workday. There are plenty of tracks for trains to "lay over" here for several hours, but be close enough to the downtown stations for the evening commute back home.

18TH STREET STATION
(Milepost 2.2) (41.8600° N, 87.6186° W)

South of the train yard lies Metra's 18th Street Station. It is almost used exclusively by Metra trains, however on rare occasion a South Shore train will stop here (mainly when there is a home Chicago Bears football game).

Metra's 18th Street Station (Public domain image)

ST. CHARLES AIR LINE
(Milepost 2.4) (41.8600° N, 87.6186° W)

A short distance south of the 18th Street Station, look west to see an elevated rail line. These tracks are part of the St. Charles Air Line, owned today by Canadian National. This rail line will cross over our electrified tracks when we are underneath McCormick Place in a minute or two. Freight trains use this line to travel between various yards in Chicago and points to the south such as Carbondale, Memphis, and New Orleans. This line is used by six Amtrak passenger trains a day, including the *City of New Orleans*, *Saluki*, and *Illini*. This line was owned by the Illinois Central, but was never electrified because its use was for freight and steam/diesel passenger service. The tracks used by our South Shore train will run parallel to this line until Kensington.

Between Randolph Street and this area, you may have noticed a limited access road paralleling our train line down in the trench. It's situated west of the tracks here, but was also east of the tracks (north of 8th Street). This 2.5-mile stretch of road is the McCormick Place Busway; it opened in 2002 at a cost of $43 million. It was meant to provide a fast way for buses to move visitors between downtown hotels and the convention center. It is also used by buses to Soldier Field sporting events, public safety workers, Metra, convention contractors, and certain government officials. Some mayors and high-ranking Chicago officials have used it to avoid downtown traffic – leaving those stuck in traffic to dub it the "mayor's road".

McCORMICK PLACE / 23RD STREET
(Milepost 2.7) (41.8579° N, 87.6189° W)

Aerial view of McCormick Place
(Public domain photo)

Just ahead, our South Shore Line train will pass underneath McCormick Place, the largest convention center in North America. It consists of four interconnected buildings that contain 2.67 million square feet of exhibit hall floor space. McCormick Place hosts numerous trade shows and meetings every year. The largest events are the Chicago Auto Show each February, the International Home/Housewares Show each March, and the National Restaurant Association Show in May. Construction began in 1958; it was opened in November 1960.

McCormick Place is a stop for South Shore Line trains on weekends only; Metra's Electric Service stops here more frequently.

Train platform at McCormick Place
(Public domain photo)

McCormick Place is named after Robert R. McCormick, a prominent member of the family of McCormick Reaper fame, and publisher of the *Chicago Tribune* newspaper. He began to promote the idea for a lakefront convention center as early as 1927. McCormick never saw his efforts pay off, passing away in 1955, three years before ground was broken.

Robert R. McCormick, 1880-1955
(Public domain photo)

Just south of McCormick Place, our tracks emerge into daylight once again. It is here we cross the beginnings of Interstate Highway 55, which stretches 964 miles south of this point, to an area just outside of New Orleans, Louisiana.

I-55 begins just south of Downtown Chicago (Public domain photo)

In Illinois, Interstate 55 replaced U.S. Route 66 as the primary highway between Chicago and St. Louis, Missouri. Even though Old Route 66 was decommissioned in the 1980's, a lot of nostalgic drivers love the alternative. South of St. Louis, I-55 travels via Arkansas, Tennessee, and Mississippi en route to the "Big Easy".

27TH STREET
(Milepost 3.2) (41.8441° N, 87.6131° W)

27th Street Metra Rail Station (Public domain photo)

Look towards the east between 25th Street and 31st Street, and you will get a glimpse of one of the many massive parking lots for McCormick Place. There are three parking lots for the convention center here, featuring a total of 5,800 parking spaces. Some of the lots around here are also used for storage of equipment and semi-trailers that carry exhibit show payloads.

27th Street is also a station stop for Metra's rail service; however, our South Shore Line train will continue to fly past. Our next station stop will be in about 30 more blocks – at 57th Street.

31ST STREET HARBOR
(Milepost 3.6) (41.8383° N, 87.6109° W)

Aerial view of the 31st Street Harbor (Public domain photo)

Between 31st Street and 35th Street, our rail line passes just to the west of 31st Street Harbor. It is the newest addition to the Chicago harbor system. Completed in 2012 with slips for 1,000 boats and a sustainable, eco-friendly design unrivaled in the industry, it provides an exceptional experience for boaters. All slips include metered electric, water (seasonal charge), and complimentary cable TV and Internet access and can accommodate boats from 35 to 70 feet in length.

Aerial view of the rail line and the 31st Street Harbor
(Public domain image)

39TH STREET
(Milepost 4.6) (41.8243° N, 87.6018° W)

📷 Near 39th Street, our train begins traveling closer to the shore of Lake Michigan. Looking to the east, passengers might get a glimpse of people enjoying the day in popular Burnham Park; it lies along a six-mile-long stretch of Lake Michigan shoreline, and connects Grant Park and Jackson Park. Burnham Park is part of the Chicago Park District. It was named after urban planner and architect Daniel Burnham; he was one of the designers of the 1893 World's Columbian Exposition and Union Station.

Enjoying the day in Burnham Park
(Public domain photo)

⛴ Chicago's famed Lake Shore Drive can also be seen passing through Burnham Park.

*South Lake Shore Drive in Chicago
(Public domain image)*

Lake Shore Drive's origins date back to Potter Palmer, who convinced the city to build a street adjacent to his lakefront property to enhance its value. Palmer built his "castle" at 1350 N. Lake Shore Drive in 1882. The drive was originally intended for leisurely strolls for the wealthy in their carriages, but as the auto age dawned, it took on a different role completely. Today, Lake Shore Drive, nicknamed 'LSD' by some, is a 16-mile highway that runs from the north side of Chicago through to the south side. Several films based in Chicago feature scenes along Lake Shore Drive, including *Cheaper by the Dozen, Ferris Bueller's Day Off, The Blues Brothers, The Break-Up, Risky Business, Love Jones, My Best Friend's Wedding, Somewhere in Time,* and *National Lampoon's Vacation.* In *When Harry Met Sally*, the title characters are seen taking Lake Shore Drive in the opposite compass direction to that which their origin point and destination would require.

△ This is also probably a good time in this reference manual to mention Lake Michigan, which can be seen east of our train line. We will parallel the lake's shoreline to Michigan City, but this is one of the best views of the lake itself that passengers get on the route.

*Map showing Lake Michigan / The Great Lakes
(Public domain photo)*

Lake Michigan is one of the five Great Lakes, but the only one that is located entirely within the United States. It is the second-largest in terms of water volume and the third-largest by surface area; it is slightly smaller than the State of West Virginia. Lake Michigan is bordered by Wisconsin, Illinois, Indiana, and Michigan. The St. Lawrence Seaway opened up the Great Lakes to ocean-going ships. Ports along its shores include Chicago, Illinois; Milwaukee, Wisconsin; Green Bay, Wisconsin; Gary, Indiana; and Benton Harbor, Michigan. In the earliest European maps of the region, the name Lake Illinois had been found in addition to that of "Michigan". It is believed to come from the Ojibwa word *mishigami* – meaning "great water".

*Sand dunes on the shore of Lake Michigan
(Public domain photo)*

43RD STREET
(Milepost 5.2) (41.8169° N, 87.5962° W)

Pedestrian walkway over the tracks at 43rd St.
(Public domain photo)

A walkway for pedestrians can be seen crossing the tracks at 43rd Street; this is used by local residents who live in Bronzeville to access the lakefront. Bronzeville is one of Chicago's many neighborhoods that we pass through on the train. In the early 20th Century, Bronzeville was known as the "Black Metropolis", one of the United States' most significant areas of African-American urban history. Between 1910 and 1920, during the peak of the "Great Migration", the population of the area increased dramatically when tens of thousands of African Americans escaped the oppression of the South and moved up to Chicago in search of industrial jobs. Since the 1950's though, population has been in a severe decline in Bronzeville.

Some famous faces once called the Bronzeville Neighborhood home. In fact, 43rd Street just west of the railroad tracks, has been designated as 'Muddy Waters Drive'. The famous blues musician, who is often cited as the "father of modern Chicago blues", lived close to the tracks here. And just one block south on 44th Street? That is where none other than Louis Armstrong called home during the 1920's. Nicknamed 'Satchmo' or 'Pops', the American trumpeter, composer, and singer was one of the most influential figures in Jazz.

Louis Armstrong once lived on 44th Street
(Public domain photo)

At 43rd Street, a mechanical interlocking was installed on the Illinois Central Railroad. This served for a period of time as a connection with the Chicago Junction Railway, formerly serving the Union Stockyards. The connection became elevated around 1920, eliminating the need for the interlocking. The connection track was torn out several years ago and there is not much to see here today.

47TH STREET (KENWOOD)
(Milepost 5.9) (41.8099° N, 87.5913° W)

47th Street passes under the railroad line here
(Public domain photo)

When the tracks cross over 47th Street, a commuter station can be seen. This is only used by Metra trains; the South Shore does not stop.

Around 47th Street, we begin to pass through Chicago's Kenwood Neighborhood. It was settled in the 1850's by the wealthy who were seeking a respite from the ever increasing congestion of the city. Kenwood was once one of Chicago's most affluent neighborhoods, and it still has some of the largest single-family homes in the city. In recent years, Kenwood has received national attention as the home of one of our former United States Presidents – Barack Obama. The Obama Mansion is located at 5046 South Greenwood, about 3,000 feet west of the tracks. Obama was a U.S. Senator from Illinois and served as President from 2009 until 2017.

Obama's mansion, located in Kenwood
(Public domain photo)

Kenwood Academy High School can be seen west of the tracks between 49th Street and 51st Street (Hyde Park Blvd.). It is operated by Chicago Public Schools and was selected as one of the country's best high schools by Newsweek and US & World News magazines.

53RD STREET (HYDE PARK)
(Milepost 6.5) (41.7995° N, 87.5869° W)

Have you noticed how the train line we are traveling on has become elevated in the past mile? On May 23, 1892, the City of Chicago passed a new ordinance requiring the Illinois Central to elevate the line between 51st Street and 67th Street in preparation for the 1893 World's Columbian Exposition.

The 1893 Columbian Exposition in Chicago
(Public domain photo)

The 1893 World's Columbian Exposition was a world's fair held in Chicago to celebrate the 400th Anniversary of Christopher Columbus' arrival in the New World in 1492. The iconic centerpiece of the Fair, the large water pool, represented the long voyage Columbus took to the New World. Chicago beat out New York City, Washington, D.C., and St. Louis for the honor of hosting the fair. The Exposition was held in Jackson Park, which is located along Chicago's lakefront, southeast of the tracks.

Back when the Illinois Central ran the commuter train operations on this line, electric "Hyde Park Local" trains made stops every four blocks north of here into Downtown Chicago. There was a tower at 51st Street that controlled the electric interlocking that was installed here back in 1926. Six tracks existed north of here, and this tower controlled the transition of rail traffic to four tracks south of here. The tower was removed in 1963, and today, the commuter line is four tracks both north and south of 51st Street. Some crossovers were retained at the site of the former tower; these were controlled remotely from 67th Street, until that practice was put to an end in 2009.

57TH STREET
(Milepost 7.0) (41.7915° N, 87.5879° W)

57th Street is a station stop on the South Shore Line for passengers visiting the Museum of Science and Industry and other attractions on the south side of Chicago. Our eastbound train continues to just board passengers here who will travel to stops in Indiana; those looking to take the train here from Downtown Chicago must use the local Metra Electric service.

Chicago's Museum of Science and Industry (Public domain photo)

The Museum of Science and Industry can be seen just to the east of the tracks near 57th Street. It is housed in the former Palace of Fine Arts, which was built for the 1893 World's Columbian Exposition. This is one of just two buildings that still exist from the Fair, due to the fact the structures were designed to be temporary. Among its diverse and expansive exhibits, the museum features a full-size replica coal mine, German submarine U-505 (captured during World War II), a 3,500-square foot model railroad, the very first diesel-powered streamlined stainless-steel passenger train (*Pioneer Zephyr*), and the Apollo 8 spacecraft that carried the first humans to orbit the moon. For over 55 years, admission to the MSI was free. Fees began to be charged during the early 1990's, with general admission rates increasing to $18 in 2015.

59TH STREET / UNIV. OF CHICAGO
(Milepost 7.4) (41.7877° N, 87.5887° W)

About two blocks south of the museum, the train passes near the University of Chicago. The campus is located west of the tracks from 57th Street to 61st Street. This private research university was established in 1890; it currently has around 15,700 students. Notable alumni include Supreme Court Justice John Paul Stevens and Astronomer Carl Sagan. With an estimated completion date of 2020, the Barack Obama Presidential Center will be housed at the university, including a presidential library.

63RD STREET
(Milepost 7.9) (41.7806° N, 87.5904° W)

Just south of 63rd Street, Mt. Carmel High School can be seen east of the tracks. About 850 students attend this all boys Catholic high school operated by the Catholic Archdiocese of Chicago. The school has been operated by the Carmelite order of priests and brothers since 1900. Notice the football field from the train? Numerous alumni have gone on to careers in the National Football League such as Donovan McNabb and Simeon Rice. 63rd Street is a flag stop for a few weekday South Shore Line trains.

67TH STREET
(Milepost 8.1) (41.7732° N, 87.5921° W)

Just south of 67th Street, look to the west of the tracks for a quick view of Oak Woods Cemetery. It covers 183 acres and was established as a 'final resting place' in 1853; the first burials took place here in 1860. Soon after the Civil War, several thousand Confederate soldiers, prisoners who died at Camp Douglas, were buried here. A monument located on the property says that 6,000 soldiers were buried here and lists the names of more than 4,000.

Our former Illinois Central railroad line remains elevated here thanks to an ordinance passed by the City of Chicago on September 29, 1902. In hopes of relieving congestion, it required the elevation of all tracks on the Illinois Central between 67th Street and 79th Street by December 1907 (the deadline was later extended until December 1912).

SOUTH CHICAGO BRANCH
(Milepost 8.2) (41.7707° N, 87.5926° W)

Around 68th Street, the South Chicago Branch of Metra breaks off the main commuter line and heads southeast.

The end of the South Chicago Branch
(Public domain photo)

The Illinois Central operated the South Chicago Branch from startup in 1883 until the line was sold to Metra in 1987. Like the main commuter line, the South Chicago Branch was electrified in 1926. In 2001, Metra built the 93rd Street terminus as a replacement for the 91st Street (South Chicago) terminal. One interesting fact about this line is that it is the only outbound Metra rail terminus located within the Chicago city limits. The line provides services to the South Chicago, South Deering, Hegewisch, and East Side Neighborhoods.

75TH STREET/GRAND CROSSING
(Milepost 9.3) (41.7574° N, 87.5956° W)

A historical view of Grand Crossing (1902)
(Public domain photo)

Just south of 75th Street, our train goes through an important railroad junction on the south side of Chicago known as Grand Crossing. For many years after its completion, the tracks at Grand Crossing intersected each other. However, during the early 1910's, the crossover bridges were built between the lines in hopes of easing train traffic congestion.

Today, this is where the Metra Electric line (used by our South Shore Line train for another five miles or so) and the Canadian National's ex-Illinois Central main line (paralleling our rail line towards the east) pass underneath two other separate, but parallel railroad bridges.

For southbound passengers, the first bridge that crosses over our tracks was the main line for the New York Central. Most of the rails have been removed and no trains use this bridge anymore. The second bridge that crosses over our route currently contains four tracks; it is owned by the Norfolk Southern and is used by numerous freight trains, as well as Amtrak's *Lake Shore Limited*, *Capitol Limited*, *Wolverine Service*, *Blue Water*, and *Pere Marquette*.

There are some interesting old-time railroad stories involving Chicago's Grand Crossing; the most infamous dates back to early 1850's. Around that time in history, many railroads in Illinois were heavily competing against each other to establish new rail lines. This was the case between the Illinois Central and the Lake Shore and Michigan Southern Railway (their mainline went from Buffalo, NY to Chicago). Instead of cooperating at railroad junction points, like all railroads do today in the interest of safety, both the IC and the LS&MS ran through Grand Crossing essentially pretending the other didn't exist. Remember, at that time, there were no bridges here at the crossing – and all tracks actually intersected. These reckless actions resulted in a crash that killed 18 people on the evening of April 25, 1853. A further investigation revealed that one of the engineers failed to observe a stop signal and was running without a headlight. Most of those killed were German immigrants who were coming to the City of Chicago to seek work and a better life.

The above historical map from the late 1800's shows the area around Grand Crossing. None of the three railroads shown passing through the junction exist today. The Chicago commuter operations of the ex-Illinois Central became part of Metra in the late 1980's. The Illinois Central ceased to exist in 1998 when the Canadian National took over freight operations. The Lake Shore & Michigan Southern Railway was merged with other rail lines in 1914 to form the New York Central. In 1968, the New York Central merged into Penn Central, and in 1976 it became part of Conrail. In 1998, the rail line became under Norfolk Southern ownership. Meanwhile, the Pittsburgh, Fort Wayne and Chicago Railway became part of Pennsylvania Railroad in the 1870's. This was merged into the Penn Central in 1968 and followed the same later ownership pattern outlined above. Since the Penn Central did not need two parallel rail lines through Grand Crossing following the 1968 merger, they decided to abandon the ex-New York Central trackage.

Just after Grand Crossing, our train will pass underneath the Chicago Skyway.

Interstate 90, the Chicago Skyway (Public domain photo)

The Chicago Skyway was built in the 1950's as a short-cut connection between the Indiana Toll Road and the Dan Ryan Expressway. The Chicago Skyway is also part of Interstate 90; at 3,020 miles, it is the longest interstate highway in the United States – connecting Boston with Seattle, Washington.

79TH STREET/CHATHAM
(Milepost 10.0) (41.7513° N, 87.5969° W)

Between 79th Street and 87th Street, the train will pass through a portion of Chicago's Chatham Neighborhood. This has been a central area for Chicago's middle-class African Americans since the late 1950's, housing many city employees and other officials. Today, more than 98% of residents of Chatham are African Americans.

In April 1911, in an effort to alleviate traffic congestion, the City of Chicago passed an ordinance requiring the Illinois Central to elevate its railroad line between 79th Street and 115th Street (Kensington). The work took about ten years to complete.

83RD STREET/AVALON PARK
(Milepost 10.4) (41.7440° N, 87.5986° W)

South of 83rd Street, Avalon Park is seen east of the tracks. This park includes baseball fields and tennis courts. A man by the name of Johnathon Pierce began to develop this area under the name "Pierce's Park" in 1888. A local church led an effort to change the name of the area, and in 1910 it became Avalon Park. Early settlers in the 1880's have included German and Irish railroad workers who built homes on stilts to raise them above the often flooded marshlands. A sewer system created in 1910 helped to drain the area and spawned further development. The area directly around Avalon Park experienced a major demographic change in the 1960's; the African American population went from less than one percent in 1960 to more than 83 percent in 1970.

87TH STREET/WOODRUFF
(Milepost 10.9) (41.7367° N, 87.6002° W)

An 18,000-square-foot warehouse can be seen east of the tracks between 87th and 91st Streets; it even has its own spur line for freight cars. This is the Chicago distribution center for Marigold, Inc., a company that makes various sweeteners for vendors like Pepsi and Archer Daniels Midland. The company was founded in Chicago in 1976, but the headquarters have since moved to Hammond, Indiana. More than a dozen employees remain here at the south side warehouse.

91ST STREET / CHESTERFIELD
(Milepost 11.4) (41.7294° N, 87.6018° W)

Around 91st Street, the train continues to travel through a residential area on the south side of Chicago. Single family homes and some apartment buildings can be seen both east and west of the tracks here.

The bridge over what is today 93rd Street was originally built in 1893 to allow the IC's trains to pass above an interurban railroad line owned by the Calumet Electric Street Railway.

A photo of the Calumet Electric Street Railway
(Public domain photo)

Just north of 95th Street, our train line will cross underneath another railroad bridge. The six tracks above us are owned by the Belt Railway of Chicago (BRC) and Chicago Rail Link (CRL). The BRC is the largest switching terminal railroad in the country; it is co-owned by six Class I railroads – BNSF, CSX, Norfolk Southern, Canadian National, Canadian Pacific, and Union Pacific. The larger railroads use the Belt Railway to transfer railroad freight cars between different lines in the Chicagoland area. Meanwhile, CRL is a shortline railroad, owned by OmniTRAX, which operates 72 miles of track on the south side of Chicago.

95TH STREET / CHICAGO STATE UNIV.
(Milepost 12.0) (41.7220° N, 87.6038° W)

The campus of Chicago State University is visible from the train, west of the tracks, between 95th and 99th Streets.

Chicago State University
(Public domain photo)

Chicago State University was founded in 1867 and has about 3,500 students; it is one of eight different public state universities in Illinois. Due to an ongoing budget stalemate in the state, about 40 percent of the staff was laid off just before the start of the 2016-17 school year. University officials say they have no plans to shut down the campus, but significant changes may be coming, since about 30 percent of the school's funding comes from state taxpayers.

99TH STREET / JAYS POTATO CHIPS
(Milepost 12.6) (41.7142° N, 87.6054° W)

Immediately before crossing the Bishop Ford Expressway, passengers should look east for the former home of Jays Potato Chips. The 126,000-square-foot building, which stands at 825 East 99th Street, is now home to several different tenants, including a company that provides phone and cable TV service and a supplier of refrigeration, heating, and cooling equipment.

*A building on 99th Street, as seen when it was home to Jays Potato Chips
(Public domain image)*

In 1927, after a series of odd jobs, including prizefighter and cemetery plot salesman, Leonard Japp turned to snack food. He created the modern-day Jays potato chip by frying potatoes in oil rather than lard, making the taste we have come to recognize: thin, crunchy, and deep-fried. The story of how Japp went from street peddler to factory owner includes none other than Al Capone, who encouraged Japp to open factories and mass-produce his snacks for Capone's speakeasies. The potato chip entered the trade about a year later, when Capone urged Japp to make them after tasting them in Sarasota, New York, where potato chips were first invented. The name of the company was changed to Jays in 1941 due to anti-Japanese sentiment during World War II.

The factory here closed in 2007, when Jays was sold to the food distributor Snyder's.

▲ Between 99th and 100th Street, the train crosses Bishop Ford Freeway. This busy stretch of road was named after Bishop Louis Henry Ford, an influential south side clergyman. Bishop Ford began as a street preacher and ended up becoming a religious and political powerhouse, a man who had the ear of mayors and even presidents. He rose to become the international leader of the Church of God in Christ, the world's largest African-American Pentecostal denomination with more than six million members. Bishop Ford Freeway is part of I-94, which runs from Michigan to Montana.

103ᴿᴰ STREET / ROSEMOOR
(Milepost 13.1) (41.7074° N, 87.6069° W)

The area around 103rd Street is known as the Rosemoor and Roseland Neighborhoods of Chicago. The area was settled in the 1840's by Dutch immigrants, who called the area "de Hooge Prairie", or the High Prairie, because it was built on higher, drier ground than the earlier Dutch settlements several miles further south.

First Reformed Church of Roseland
(Public domain photo)

The community was farm-based until the late 19th Century, when the nearby town of Pullman was built between Roseland and Lake Calumet; residents then began taking jobs in the nearby factories. Roseland was annexed into Chicago by 1892, as the farmland transformed into a commercial and residential community. The thriving fortunes of the area began to change in the 1960's when industry patterns lead to economic decline. Sadly, Roseland has yet to recover from businesses being shuttered and gang violence.

PULLMAN NATIONAL MONUMENT
(Milepost 14.0) (41.6947° N, 87.6099° W)

Between 109th and 115th Streets passengers should look east for a quick view of Pullman National Monument, a new unit of the National Park Service. The most pronounced building is the large clock tower that was once part of the administration and factory complex (photos on the next two pages).

George Pullman was born in New York and studied engineering. He came to Chicago in the 1850's and designed a method used to raise buildings, which allowed for better drainage and cut down on the horrid sanitation issues the city was facing. He utilized his accumulated wealth and founded the Pullman Palace Car Company in 1867 to manufacture railroad sleeping cars. Through a focus on customer comfort and luxury, Pullman gained a larger market in the railroad car sector.

When demand increased in 1880, Pullman not only built a brand new factory, but an entire community for his workers. He established behavioral standards that workers had to meet and charged them rent. The distinctive row houses were comfortable by standards of the day, and contained such amenities as indoor plumbing, gas, and sewers.

Renovated Pullman Row Houses
(Public domain photo)

An aerial view of the rail line used by our train (right) and Pullman National Monument (left)

Pullman maintained control and ownership of everything in town – including choosing which stores could be established, which books the library could offer, and which performances could appear in the theater. He even assumed his residents would be satisfied with one church and a form of worship chosen by Pullman himself – the Greenstone Church. Pullman did not allow residents to own their own homes. Residents were also strictly prohibited from consuming alcoholic beverages; the town had one tavern that only served visitors. Pullman even went as far as hiring spies or "spotters" to watch for and report any resident who behaved contrary to his policies. This caused some to leave Pullman and buy homes in nearby areas like Roseland and Gano.

During the early-to-mid-1890's, the country was in a nationwide depression. When orders for new sleeping cars began to fall, Pullman decided to reduce workers' wages without reducing rents, utility charges, or store prices. Residents asked for reduced rents, but when their pleas fell on deaf ears, members of the American Railway Union went on strike in 1894. It lasted for two months, eventually leading to intervention by the U.S. government and military. After George Pullman died in 1897, the Illinois Supreme Court required the company to sell the town because operating it was outside the company's charter. Many of the workers ended up simply buying their homes; Pullman gradually was absorbed as a regular Chicago neighborhood.

With industrial and railroad restructuring beginning in the 1950's, many jobs were lost in this area of the city. By 1969, the Pullman Company was dissolved and all assets were liquidated. The Historic Pullman Foundation was formed in 1973 to preserve and restore the remaining factory buildings and homes. President Obama established Pullman National Monument in 2015, creating the first National Park Service unit in the Chicagoland area.

The Pullman Chicago Clock Tower can be seen from the train   (Public domain image)

115TH STREET/KENSINGTON
(Milepost 14.5/75.5)(41.6854° N, 87.6120° W)

CN Tracks seen from 115th St. Metra platform (Public domain photo)

Born as a railroad town named Calumet Junction, Kensington was founded where the Illinois Central and Michigan Central railroad connected in 1852. The town grew slowly until, by 1880, 400 German, Irish, Scandinavian, and American residents lived there, servicing the railroads and the population of farmers in the vicinity. Despite the presence of churches, stores, and schools, Kensington became very notorious for saloons, leading the Dutch in Roseland to nickname it "Bumtown". Even though it was its own neighborhood, residents had a strong connection with Pullman. Some Pullman factory workers lived in Kensington and Kensington businessmen lived in Pullman. As industries began to close in the 1960's and 1970's, Kensington's population also began to change. Mexicans and African Americans returned for the first time since the 1920's; by 1980 African Americans came to dominate the community. Kensington was a stop for South Shore trains until 2012.

Immediately south of the 115th Street – Kensington station, our South Shore train will leave the Metra Electric Line we have been sharing for the past 14.5 miles with Metra since Millennium Station in Downtown Chicago.

Our train will swing to the southeast here, crossing over two north-south tracks without overhead electrified wires. Once again, this is the former Illinois Central main line for freight and long-distance trains that used either steam or diesel locomotives. Today, this is owned by Canadian National Railway. Amtrak passenger trains to Carbondale, Memphis, and New Orleans use this line. Obviously, South Shore trains must get clearance also from the CN dispatcher that no trains are coming in order to cross over these two busy tracks.

An electric interlocking was installed here at Kensington in 1909 and 1918. Additionally, a mechanical interlocking, in 1982, was installed here as well. In 1926, a new tower was constructed here that remained in use until September 8, 2007.

Map of the rail lines at Kensington (Public domain photo)

Now that our eastbound train is done using Metra and is operating tracks owned by the South Shore, there will be a change in milepost measurements. While on Metra, distances were measured by how far a train was from Millennium Station. Kensington is 14.5 miles from Millennium Station, hence Milepost 14.5. The South Shore measures distance based on how far a train is from South Bend Airport. Kensington is 75.5 miles from the Airport.

Passengers get a glimpse of the historic Illinois Central Tower at Kensington
(Public domain image)

At time of publication, the historic Illinois Central control tower at Kensington still stands; it can be seen east of the tracks just before crossing East Kensington Avenue – and just before the South Shore breaks off from Metra.

The tower was built by the Illinois Central as part of their electric line improvements in the 1920's. Up through the early part of the 21st century the Metra Electric division was still primarily a tower controlled line with control locations at Randolph Street Station (some sort of panel), Weldon Yard (non-interlocked with switch-tenders on all main tracks), 67th St (GRS model 5 electro-mechanical) and Kensington (CTC and direct wire panel). Metra first moved control of Randolph St into its central control room, followed by Kensington and its territory and finally in March 2009, 67th Street was cut over. The non-interlocked portion between Van Buren and Roosevelt is still controlled by switchtenders and of those three closed towers, only 67th St was technically re-signaled as its interlocking was electro-mechanical, not relay like the others.

SHERWIN-WILLIAMS PLANT

Photos of the Sherwin-Williams Plant in Chicago's Riverdale Neighborhood
(Public domain photos)

In the general vicinity of the Kensington station, the train will pass by a plant owned by Sherwin-Williams; it can be seen just to the east of the South Shore railroad line.

The story of The Sherwin-Williams Company began in 1866, when Henry Sherwin used his life savings of $2,000 to buy a partnership in the Truman Dunham Company of Ohio. The firm was a distributor of pigments, painting supplies, oils, and glass. In four years, this original partnership was dissolved, and Sherwin organized a paint business with new partners, Edward P. Williams and A. T. Osborn. The new business was called Sherwin-Williams & Company.

In 1888, the company saw the possibility of marketing paints and coatings to the railroad industry. It opened a manufacturing facility in Chicago to serve the Pullman Company and to better serve the farm-implement and carriage industries. In those days, Pullman required as many as 20 coats of high-quality finishes for the elaborate interiors of the Pullman cars. Sherwin hired George A. Martin, an ambitious young man, to run the new facility. He later would go on to become company president.

Today, the Sherwin-Williams facility that can be seen from South Shore trains contains two active divisions. The Chicago Emulsions Plant (CEP) manufactures water-based latex coatings, and the Steudel Center is a coatings research and development facility.

Other shut down areas of the plant can also be seen from the train. The former Paint Plant (deactivated in May 1997) produced organic solvent-based paints and special purpose coatings. The former Resin Plant operations (deactivated in 1992) manufactured resins to be used as raw materials in the manufacturing process of paint.

If you notice some rolling hills around this area (especially to the east), they are not natural; these are former landfill sites. Since the mid-1980's, Chicago has had a ban on new and expanded landfills. Land and Lakes Company last used the landfill located east of the tracks in the mid-1990's.

RIVERDALE NEIGHBORHOOD

For the next few miles, we will travel through Chicago's Riverdale Neighborhood. The first non-native settler in the area was David Perriam who, in 1837, claimed land north of the horseshoe bend in the Calmuet River in an area referred to as Wildwood. This land was later acquired by Colonel James H. Bowen who was instrumental in construction of the Cal-Sag canal, connecting the Calumet River to the Illinois River. After he lost his home in the Chicago Fire, Bowen moved to Wildwood and made this a palatial summer home where Chicago's elite gathered in the 1870's. However, over time, wealthy residents began to prefer to live along the lakefront, and since the riverfront areas had more exposure to industrial pollution, they were left to the poor. Various industries moved to this area – and in fact, more people worked here in Riverdale than lived here for quite a long period of time. In the 1960's and 1970's, the area's industries began to close and the population increased and became mostly African American. In fact, the 2010 census report shows more than 96% of the population is now African American.

Chicago's Riverdale Neighborhood
(Public domain image)

CALUMET RECLAMATION PLANT
(Milepost 74.3) (41.6659° N, 87.5996° W)

For the next almost one mile, we will be traveling by the Calumet Water Reclamation Plant; it can be seen on both sides of the train. This is the oldest of seven wastewater treatment facilities in the Chicagoland area; it opened in 1922 and serves just about one million people today. Workers treat upwards of 480 million gallons of wastewater per day, which is collected from an area of around 300 square miles in Chicago and its southern suburbs.

Our train will pass by the Calumet Reclamation Plant's sewer sludge drying area; this can be seen by looking out the east side windows.

Sewer sludge can be seen from the train
(Public domain image)

So what is going on at the plant and what are the muddy looking fields here? Let's start at the beginning to understand the whole process a little better. Both wastewater and storm water enter the sewage system and flow to Chicago's Calumet Reclamation Plant. Included is anything flushed down the toilet or dumped down the drain in homes, schools, hospitals, streets, businesses, or industries. Workers at the treatment plant then clean the liquid part of the sewage and attempt to remove some of the toxic metals, excess nutrients and pathogens from the wastewater. The resulting liquid is discharged into nearby Lake Calumet as 'effluent'.

The leftover solids and semi-solids that are filtered from wastewater make up what is called 'sewer sludge'. This is what you are seeing from the train – basically large beds of 'sewer sludge'. This material is air dried and aged on these large outdoor drying beds; they rest on six inches of asphalt, which prevent the sewer sludge from mixing with the earth and ground water, which would add to the drying time. About 2,600 tons of water per acre is evaporated from these beds annually. Material here is generally turned once every two days to expose wetter material to air and sun to speed drying. After the solids have been dried, they are hauled by truck or barge to various locations where they are put back into the soil.

Sewer sludge is typically treated to remove some, but not all, of the contaminants. In recent decades, the sludge lobby (yes, there is one) has rebranded the treated sludge as 'bio-solids'. Sludge is applied to farmland – or even golf courses, home gardens, and in the past, even the White House lawn. Various cities get very creative at branding their sludge, so gardeners can choose between 'Hou-Actinite' from the Houston area, 'Milorganite' from Milwaukee, or 'GroCo' from Seattle.

Aerial map of the plant
(Public domain image)

So what happens to the remaining contaminants in the sewer sludge when they are applied to the soil? Well, that is really anyone's guess. Some chemicals bind to the soil; others do not. Some chemicals leach into groundwater and others are insoluble in water. Because of some of the uncertainties, the practice of growing food in soil treated with the sewer sludge, has become controversial. Currently, numerous companies, such as Del Monte, Heinz, Kraft, and others have policies that prohibit using produce grown on land that has been sprayed with this sludge.

To be fair, we have to mention that there are groups who promote the use of farmers using sewer sludge, too. Some scientists and waste experts say the use of sewer sludge helps the environment by returning valuable nutrients, like nitrogen, back to the land. They say people are just squeamish from using a product made from human waste, even if it's heavily treated.

CALUMET RIVER
(Milepost 72.6) (41.6581° N, 87.5723° W)

After passing by the south end of the waste treatment plant, our train line will make a curve, as we begin traveling due east now. Our train will cross over I-94 again, which is still designated the Bishop Ford Expressway here. A short distance later, the train crosses a truss bridge over the Calumet River.

South Shore Line Bridge over Calumet River
(Public domain image)

The original bridge was built by the Chicago South Shore & South Bend Railroad in 1906; it was re-built in 1966. The name 'Calumet' is from the French colonial name for a particular type of ceremonial pipe used by Native Americans; it served as a universal sign of peace among the Illiniwek, and which was presented to Pere Marquette in 1673.

Photo of a calumet
(Public domain image)

The Calumet river system is actually a network of waterways; some are human-made and others are natural, but have been transformed by two centuries of human straightening, widening, dredging, channelizing, and damming. Industrial pollution and landfilling of nearby marshes have also changed how the river now appears and where it is located.

HEGEWISCH NEIGHBORHOOD

Near the crossing of the Calumet River, our eastbound train begins to travel through a neighborhood of Chicago called Hegewisch. It was supposed to be a company town for the United States Rolling Stock Company, a business that was going to build rail cars for railroad companies. The man in charge of laying out the town was Adolph Hegewisch. He was no stranger to railroads or rail supply companies, having spent several decades in managing rail lines and sitting on the boards of many east coast rail companies. Hegewisch knew that if his company was to have any chance of success it would need to be located in an area that showed great potential for railroad growth. The area he chose in 1883 was an area where more than half-a-dozen different rail lines met before heading north to Chicago. Hegewisch planned to build his company town right in the middle of this important junction.

Due to a lack of capital, these plans for the company never came to fruition, and the town of Hegewisch fell dramatically short of its estimate of 10,000 residents by 1885 – only 500 names were listed in the town directory four years later.

In 1889, Hegewisch was annexed to Chicago along with the rest of Hyde Park Township. Adolph died a few years later and the Rolling Stock Company became part of the Pressed Steel Car Company before World War I. During these decades, Joseph H. Brown and other industrialists developed steel mills in and around Hegewisch. New residents included many Polish, Yugoslavian, Czechoslovakian, Swedish, and Irish workers.

Historic post card for Hegewisch
(Public domain image)

The steel mills around Hegewisch remained the mainstays of the community over the next half century. The Pressed Steel Car Company switched its manufacturing operation from railroad cars to Howitzer tanks and other vehicles during World War II.

After the Vietnam War, steel manufacturing waned across America, Hegewisch included. After the closure of Wisconsin Steel in 1980, the population declined because of layoffs. Since then, Hegewisch has balanced out some of its population losses with the relocation of a significant number of Mexican-Americans into the area.

HEGEWISCH MARSH
(Milepost 72.1) (41.6582° N, 87.5678° W)

Almost immediately after the train crosses the Calumet River, look out the south side windows for a view of Hegewisch Marsh.

A view of Hegwisch Marsh
(Public domain image)

Hegewisch Marsh is a premiere site for wetland birds. A small colony of yellow-headed blackbirds nest and fledge their young here each year. In the years before Northeastern Illinois' wetlands were drained and filled, yellow-headed blackbirds were common residents of local marshes. They are now listed as an endangered species in Illinois. Hegewisch Marsh is also a nesting site for pied-billed grebes and common moorhen, both of which are threatened species in Illinois. Best times to see birds from the train are in the early morning and evening; during the heat of the day, the birds tend to remain in the denser cattails.

FORD MOTOR COMPANY CHICAGO ASSEMBLY PLANT
(Milepost 71.9) (41.6580° N, 87.5594° W)

After passing through Hegewisch Marsh, the train will go over a bridge – passing above a double-tracked Norfolk Southern railroad line and Torrence Avenue. Located just north of here is the Ford Motor Company's Chicago Assembly Plant, frequently called Torrence Avenue Assembly.

A photo taken inside the Ford Plant
(Public domain image)

This facility on the south side of Chicago is Ford's oldest continually-operated automobile manufacturing plant in the world. Workers here are currently responsible for production of the Ford Taurus and the Ford Explorer, both of which share the same platform. Just over 4,000 workers are employed here.

Production started on March 3, 1924, as an alternative production site for the Model T to the River Rouge Plant in Michigan. It switched to Model A production in 1928, and built M8 Greyhound and M20 Armored Utility Car armored cars during World War II. It was the site of pickup truck production for 40 years before that operation stopped in 1964. In 1985, it was selected as the site of production for the Ford Taurus and Mercury Sable midsize sedans.

Between here and the Hegewisch station, look west of the tracks for a large parking lot. Finished Ford Taurus and Ford Explorers are parking in the lot, waiting to be loaded on to Norfolk Southern freight train auto carriers. Some vehicles are also shipped by truck.

Just before arriving at the station, look to the north and east of the rail line to see an M60 tank. No, we're not under invasion; it is part of the new Hegewisch Veterans Memorial. It was moved here from a fort in Alabama a few years ago and was used during the Vietnam War.

HEGEWISCH STATION
(Milepost 70.7) (41.6455° N, 87.5424° W)

Two photos of South Shore Hegewisch Station (Public domain image)

Hegewisch is the South Shore Line's easternmost stop in Chicago and the last one in Illinois outbound, and offers pay parking. It is the only Illinois station on the South Shore Line not shared with the Metra Electric Line. There is a unique arrangement at the station as far as fares are concerned; although this station is a South Shore Line stop and the tracks are owned by NICTD, the station and the parking lots are actually owned by Metra and thus subject to Metra's fares, because the station is within the State of Illinois. Thus, when the South Shore Line adjusts its fares, the fares for Hegewisch do not change, but if Metra adjusts its fares, the fares at Hegewisch are adjusted accordingly.

Near the station, look north and east of the tracks for a view of Calumet Harbor Lumber Company; it touts itself as the only sawmill in the City of Chicago. It has been in business for over a century. In the early 1900's there were as many as 50 sawmills within city limits.

BURNHAM JUNCTION
(Milepost 70.5) (41.6449° N, 87.5419° W)

Burnham Junction, just east of Hegewisch (Public domain image)

Just east of the Hegewisch station, our train crosses over a single-tracked north-south railroad line known as the South Chicago & Southern (sometimes called the "Bernice Cutoff"). At one time, it was a Pennsylvania Railroad line that connected their Panhandle route to the south (at Bernice Junction) with the Fort Wayne main line near Lake Michigan (Colehour Junction). Both the north and south ends of the SC&S have been abandoned, as has the Panhandle itself, but the middle segment is still in operation. This line sees only occasional traffic; Norfolk Southern and Indiana Harbor Belt locals use it to access NS's River Branch serving several industries north of here along the Calumet River. Before the north and south ends were torn up, Amtrak trains from Indianapolis used the SC&S, but when Conrail insisted on abandoning it, Amtrak reluctantly agreed.

BURNHAM YARD
(Milepost 69.9) (41.6386° N, 87.5327° W)

A South Shore Freight train in Burnham Yard (Public domain image)

Up until now, this route guide has really only discussed passenger service on the South Shore Line – but there is also a freight side.

Freight service began on this line in 1916 when the railroad was still part of the Chicago, Lake Shore and South Bend Railway. It continued to be operated under the same ownership as South Shore passenger service through the Samuel Insull era, into CSX ownership (1967-1984), and finally that of Venango River Corporation. When Venango declared bankruptcy in 1989, the Northern Indiana Commuter Transportation District (NICTD) purchased the passenger rail assets, while a company called Anacostia and Pacific bought the freight side of operations.

South Shore Freight's primary businesses are coal and steel, with the coal being delivered to the Burns Harbor and Michigan City generating stations owned by Northern Indiana Public Service Company (NIPSCO). It also serves many other customers along the line. Other materials hauled by South Shore freight trains include chemicals, grain, manufactured products, paper, pig iron, and roofing materials. South Shore Freight currently owns 12 rail locomotives and 600 freight cars.

Passengers may be able to see some freight traffic on the South Shore as we pass through Burnham Yard, located near Milepost 70. Most freight traffic will be south of our tracks, however a freight train sometimes will use the northernmost track (adjacent to Brainard Ave.).

STATE LINE JUNCTION
(Milepost 69.2) (41.6327° N, 87.5252° W)

Just before crossing the Illinois-Indiana State Line, our train will cross a single-tracked north-south branch line owned by the Indiana Harbor Belt Railroad.

An IHB branch line crosses the South Shore (Public domain image)

The Indiana Harbor Belt Railroad, which has been in operating since 1896, is owned today by Canadian Pacific, CSX, and Norfolk Southern.

The Indiana Harbor Belt main line runs from Hammond, Indiana to Franklin Park, Illinois (located on the northwest side of Chicago). The primary duty of the railroad is to switch freight rail cars between larger rail operators.

ILLINOIS-INDIANA STATE LINE
(Milepost 69.1) (41.6324° N, 87.5248° W)

APRHF Rail Rangers Guides at the State Line (Photo by Robert Tabern)

△ Just past the IHB rail crossing, our train leaves Chicago and the State of Illinois. We now begin our 69 mile journey through four counties in Northwest Indiana before reaching South Bend Airport.

What is now the state line between Illinois and Indiana was originally established by Congress as the dividing line between Illinois Territory and Indiana Territory. When Indiana Territory was established in 1800, it covered a large chunk of what is now the Upper Midwest, including present-day Indiana, Illinois, and Wisconsin, as well as the portion of Minnesota east of the Mississippi River, almost all of Michigan's Upper Peninsula, and the western half of the Lower Peninsula. Residents who began settling in the northwestern part of Indiana Territory felt they were too far from Vincennes, the territorial capital. As a result, Congress carved out Illinois Territory from the western portions of Indiana Territory in 1809. The boundary between the two was set as the Wabash River – from the Ohio River to a point south of Terre Haute – and then an imaginary line due north from there. This border was kept in place when Indiana became a state in 1816, and when Illinois became a state two years later in 1818.

Speaking of state lines, if it wasn't for a man named Nathaniel Pope, what is now Downtown Chicago could have ended up in Wisconsin. It's a story even most native-Illinoisans don't know and most proud Chicago Bears fans would probably never admit to.

The original provisions of the old Northwest Ordinance set Illinois' northern boundary equal with the southern tip of Lake Michigan. Such a boundary would have actually left Illinois with no shoreline on Lake Michigan what-so-ever.

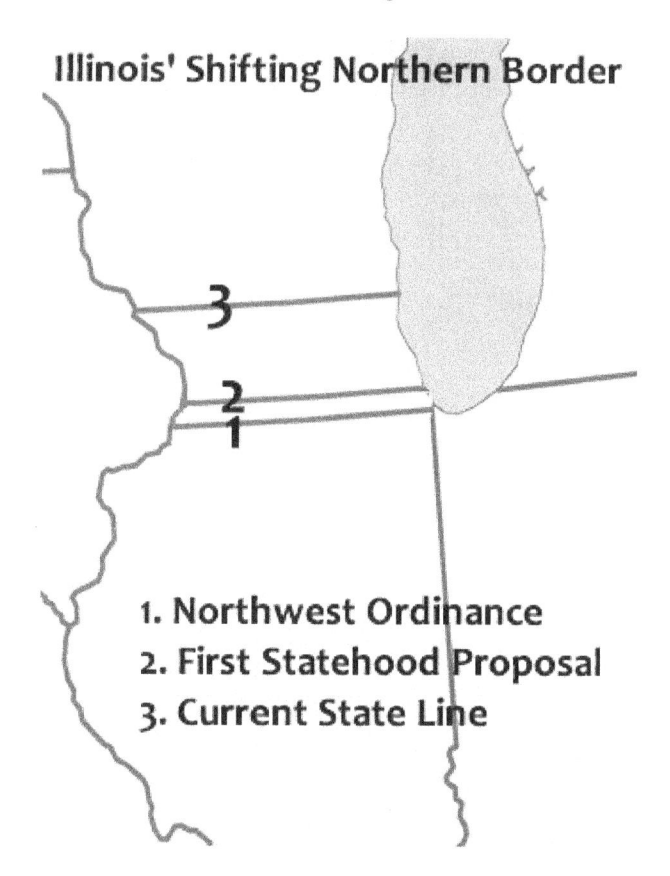

Illinois' Shifting Northern Border

1. Northwest Ordinance
2. First Statehood Proposal
3. Current State Line

When Indiana became a state in 1816, its northern border was moved ten miles north by Congress in order to give the new state some usable land adjoining the lake. Those who were drawing up the bill for Illinois' statehood in 1818 also built in a similar ten mile extension of its northern border for the same reason.

If the original bill was kept as first written, the Illinois-Wisconsin State Line would have run through the southern part of Chicago, or around where Midway Airport is located today.

Despite the northern border being moved north by ten miles, Illinois delegate Nathaniel Pope wanted even more land for his state. Pope lobbied to have the boundary moved further north, and the final bill passed by Congress did just that; it included an amendment to shift the border to 42° 30' north, which is approximately 51 miles north of Indiana's northern border. This shift added 8,500 square miles to the state, including the important lead mining region near Galena. More importantly, it added nearly 50 miles of Lake Michigan shoreline and the Chicago River. Pope and others envisioned a canal which would connect the Chicago and Illinois rivers, and thusly, connect the Great Lakes to the Mississippi River. This would go on to become the Illinois & Michigan Canal.

Nathaniel Pope
(Public domain image)

Pope tried to influence the forming of Illinois by more than just its state boundaries. Fearing that there weren't the 40,000 people needed to turn Illinois from a territory into a state, he actually tried to remove the population and census requirements from the piece of legislation creating Illinois. Pope was not successful in his efforts with this, and a census was mandated. Many question how valid the census was though for creating Illinois, with workers counting everyone they saw out on the road as a potential new resident. There are even reports that some people were counted multiple times. Regardless, Illinois did indeed become the 21st state.

LAKE COUNTY, INDIANA
(Milepost 508.3) (41.7046° N, 87.5249° W)

The Illinois-Indiana State Line also marks the point where our train leaves Cook County and enters Lake County. It was named for its location on Lake Michigan, which forms the northern border of the county. This is also the farthest northwest county in Indiana. With just under 500,000 residents, Lake County is the second largest in Indiana in terms of the population. There are 19 different cities and towns in Lake County.

HAMMOND
(Population: 78,967; Elevation: 587 feet)

The first city that our eastbound train passes through in Indiana is Hammond. The first permanent residents arrived around 1847 to settle on land between the Grand and Little Calumet Rivers, on the south end of Lake Michigan. They were German farmers newly arrived from Europe looking for land and opportunity. Before that time, the area was a crossroad for Indian tribes, explorers, stagecoach lines and supply lines to the West. A convenient location and abundant fresh water from Lake Michigan led to the beginning of Hammond's industrialization in 1869 with the George H. Hammond Company meat-packing plant following merchants and farmers to the area. Hammond was incorporated on April 21, 1884, and was named after the Detroit butcher. In 1868, Hammond received a patent for a refrigerator railcar design. In the early 1870's, he built a new plant along the tracks of the Michigan Central Railroad. By 1873, the Hammond Company was selling one million dollars' worth of meat a year; by 1875, sales were nearly two million dollars.

The Hammond Company's large packing house in Hammond rivaled those located at the Union Stock Yard in Chicago. By the middle of the 1880's, when it built a new plant in Omaha, Hammond was slaughtering over 100,000 cattle a year and owned a fleet of 800 refrigerator cars. After Hammond died in 1886, the company became less important and no longer challenged the giant Chicago packers, who acquired Hammond at the turn of the century and merged it into their National Packing Company.

HAMMOND STATION
(Milepost 68.5) (41.6309° N, 87.5152° W)

Hammond, Indiana South Shore Line stop (Public domain image)

A little more than two miles east of the Hegewisch station, our train will make a stop at the Hammond South Shore station. It consists of a pair of high-level platforms located between the crossings of Hohman and Johnson Avenues. The southern platform is a side platform serving eastbound trains to Michigan City and South Bend while the northern platform, situated between the two tracks, is of the island type but only serves westbound trains to Chicago. The tracks through the station are gauntlet tracks which permit the passage of freight trains.

A Hammond Refrigerator Line model train car (Public domain image)

🚉 Hammond's other passenger train station is located about four miles north of here, near the Horseshoe Hammond Casino and the shore of Lake Michigan. This is used by Amtrak Wolverine Service trains that operate between Chicago's Union Station and Detroit/Pontiac, Michigan.

△ Less than a ½-mile east of the Hammond South Shore Line station, the train crosses a bridge over Calumet Avenue. This is part of U.S. Route 41, a 2,000-mile-long roadway that runs between the Upper Peninsula of Michigan and Miami, Florida. U.S. Route 41 runs through the eastern half of Indiana, connecting such cities as Hammond, Kentland, Terre Haute, Vincennes, and Evansville.

U.S. Highway 41 in Indiana
(Public domain image)

🚉 About four blocks east of U.S. 41, South Shore Line trains curve to the southeast and begin running parallel to the Indiana Toll Road (Interstate 90) on an elevated right-of-way. Before the Indiana Toll Road was built in 1956, the South Shore Line kept going due east along Chicago Avenue into East Chicago. There was even a segment of "street running" for the South Shore in East Chicago, where the train would run right down the middle of the street alongside cars. It was decided re-locating the tracks along the Toll Road would create fewer traffic tie-ups and accidents.

South Shore "street running" in East Chicago
(Courtesy: Sandy Goodrick)

GRAND CALUMET RIVER
(Milepost 66.9)(41.6854° N, 87.6120° W)

South Shore bridge over Grand Calumet River
(Public domain image)

〰️ Near Milepost 67, the train will cross a bridge over the Grand Calumet River; it is 13 miles long. The majority of the river's flow drains into Lake Michigan via the Indiana Harbor and Ship Canal, sending 1,500 cubic feet per second of water into the lake. A smaller part of the flow, the river's western end, enters the Calumet River and ultimately drains into the Illinois River. Sadly, the Grand Calumet is among the country's most severely polluted. However, an effort is underway to rehabilitate the river ecosystem.

EAST CHICAGO
(Population: 29,212; Elevation: 591 feet)

*A view of Downtown East Chicago
(Public domain image)*

Near the Grand Calumet River Bridge, we briefly leave Hammond and begin passing through East Chicago. From 1893 to 1998, this city was home of the Inland Steel Company. East Chicago remains heavily industrialized, with Arcelor Mittal's Indiana Harbor Works and the Indiana Harbor Ship Canal Complex. The city got its name due to its location being southeast of Chicago, Illinois.

EAST CHICAGO STATION
(Milepost 66.3)(41.6114° N, 87.4790° W)

About two miles east of the Hammond station, our eastbound South Shore Line train will stop at the East Chicago station. East Chicago consists of a single high-level island platform situated between two gauntlet tracks which permit the passage of freight trains. The northern track provides service to Chicago while the southern track services Michigan City and South Bend. At this location the South Shore Line is situated on an embankment and the platform traverses Indianapolis Boulevard. The station building is located east of Indianapolis Boulevard at ground level. The station is staffed with a ticket agent in the morning hours and is also equipped with a ticket vending machine. Adjacent to the station is a parking lot with capacity for 1,200 cars.

*East Chicago's South Shore Line station
(Public domain image)*

BUCKEYE OIL STORAGE TERMINAL
(Milepost 65.7)(41.6105° N, 87.4668° W)

Just about one half-mile east of the East Chicago station, the train passes by several large white tanks to the south. More tanks can be seen across the Toll Road to the north, as well. The facility is owned by Buckeye Partners and is used to store diesel fuel, jet fuel, and ethanol. The fuel is brought in by pipeline from several of the local refineries in the area (such as BP in Whiting, Indiana). It is then stored here, and distributed to locations as far away as Southwestern Illinois, Ohio, and Pennsylvania. Buckeye bought this facility in 2005 from Shell. More than 1.3 million gallons of fuel can be stored here alone at Buckeye's Hammond Terminal. An oil depot is a comparatively unsophisticated facility in that there is no processing or other transformation on site. The products which reach the depot (from a refinery) are in their final form suitable for delivery to customers. In some cases, additives may be injected into products in tanks, but there is usually no manufacturing plant on site.

Aerial view of the oil tank farm
(Public domain image)

One of the tanks at Hammond
(Public domain image)

PARRISH
(Milepost 64.9)(41.6105° N, 87.4668° W)

Just east of the oil tank facility, the train crosses back into the City of Hammond. The area around here has historically been known on the South Shore Line as "Parrish". The name comes from John C. Parrish, who was a stockholder in the East Chicago Company, which was developing the city. Apparently he got a little too eager and named a street after himself. Parrish Avenue is located just north of the railroad tracks here, explaining the name.

Railroad facilities here at Parrish include a cross-over switch at Milepost 64.9, which allows trains to switch between the two main tracks if needed. There is also a railroad siding that goes into another oil tank farm facility to the south. It comes back into the main line of the South Shore around Milepost 63.9 (at a point called "Parrish Siding").

GARY
(Population: 78,450; Elevation: 587 feet)

Around Milepost 63.8, the train tracks will pass underneath Cline Avenue, a major north-south roadway. This is the point where the South Shore leaves Hammond and begins traveling through the City of Gary. It is quite large in both population and size; our train will actually travel within the Gary city limits for more than ten miles.

An aerial view of Gary's City Center
(Public domain image)

The City of Gary was founded in 1906 by the United States Steel Corporation as the home for its new plant, Gary Works. The city was named after lawyer Elbert Henry Gary, who served as the founding chairman of U.S. Steel.

Gary was the site of civil unrest in the Steel Strike of 1919. A riot broke out on Broadway, the main north-south street through Downtown Gary between steel workers who were on strike and strike breakers brought in from outside. Three days later, Governor James P. Goodrich declared martial law. Soon after, over 4,000 federal troops were brought in to restore order.

U.S. Steel in Gary, Indiana
(Public domain image)

Over the years, Gary's fortunes have risen and fallen with those of the steel industry. The growth of the steel industry brought prosperity to the community. Department stores and movie houses were built in the downtown area and the Glen Park Neighborhood. In the 1960's, like many other American urban centers reliant on one particular industry, Gary entered a spiral of decline. It has continued, even until today, thanks to growing overseas competition in the steel industry. In fact, a recent report by Gary city officials has estimated that one-third of all homes in the city are unoccupied and/or abandoned. Gary's population is currently less than half of what it was during the 1960's.

One of Gary's most notable residents was pop singer Michael Jackson; he was born here on August 29, 1958. His album, *Thriller*, remains the best-selling album of all time, with estimated sales of 65 million copies worldwide.

Michael Jackson was born in Gary, Indiana
(Public domain image)

Gary also played in a role in pop culture thanks to a certain song in Act II of the 1957 Broadway smash hit "The Music Man". Harold Hill poses as a boys' band leader who is trying to con naive Iowa townsfolk. Hill claimed that he graduated from Gary's Conservatory of Music in 1905. (Remember, Gary was not even founded until the following year!)

Part of the song goes as such:

"Gary, Indiana!
What a wonderful name,
Named for Elbert Gary of judiciary fame.
Gary, Indiana, as a Shakespeare would say,
Trips along softly on the tongue this way--
Gary, Indiana, Gary Indiana, Gary, Indiana,
Let me say it once again.
Gary, Indiana, Gary, Indiana, Gary, Indiana,
That's the town that "knew me when."

*A song about Gary, in the "Music Man"
(Public domain image)*

GARY-CHICAGO INT'L AIRPORT
(Milepost 62.9)(41.6085° N, 87.4176° W)

📷 Shortly after crossing into Gary, the train will go by Gary-Chicago International Airport, which can be seen towards the north. After opening in 1954, airport officials were hoping to attract customers who were looking for a smaller and less-crowded airport experience in Chicagoland. For a while, things were looking up as the marketing team billed Gary-Chicago as the city's "third airport" – an alternative to either O'Hare International or Midway.

The airport was once served by the now defunct Pan Am, Southeast Airlines, SkyValue Airlines, Skybus Airlines, and Hooters Air, with direct flights to destinations such as Hartford, Connecticut; St. Petersburg, Florida; Greensboro, North Carolina; and Myrtle Beach, South Carolina.

Major commercial air service came to an end at Gary-Chicago International in July 2013 when Allegiant Air ended its twice-per-week service to Orlando-Sanford International Airport. The airport is now considered to be a "dead airport", using the term to describe a lack of regular scheduled commercial passenger flights.

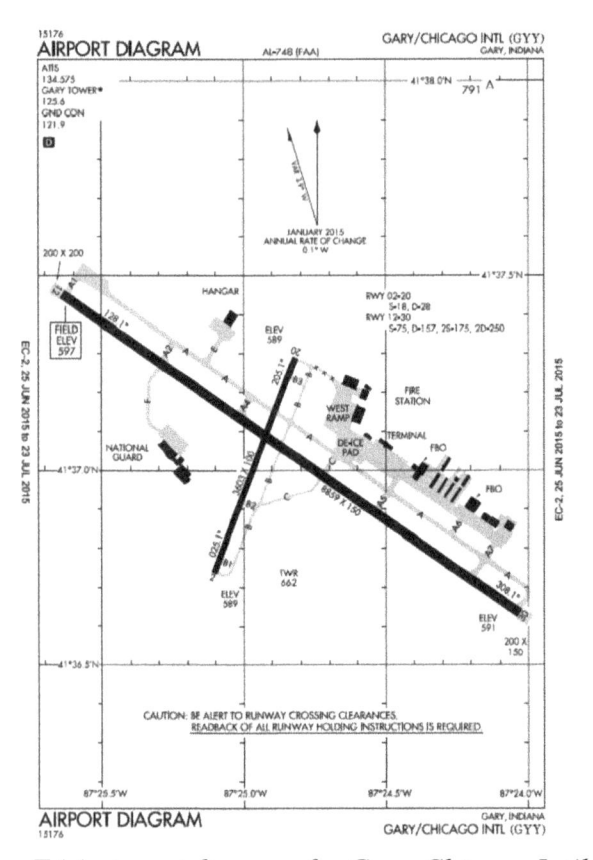

*FAA airport diagram for Gary-Chicago Int'l
(Public domain image)*

CLARK ROAD STATION
(Milepost 61.7)(41.6054° N, 87.3943° W)

About five miles east of the East Chicago station, our train stops at the Gary Airport/Clark Road station. This is the furthest western station in Gary, serving the Brunswick Neighborhood. There are two other South Shore stations in the city that we will pass later on. It also serves the airport, although it does not provide direct access to the airport. The station itself consists of a single platform north of the tracks and three Plexiglas shelters. The station is a flag stop, and passengers must alert the conductor in advance if they want to get off and must activate a strobe light flag stop signal if they want to get on. Since there are no commercial flights left, this has become the lowest ridership South Shore station in the system.

Gary Airport/Clark Road South Shore stop (Public domain image)

Just east of the station, at Milepost 61.5, is a rail point known as Clark Crossover, which allows trains to switch between the two main tracks, if needed.

GARY'S AMBRIDGE NEIGHBORHOOD

East of Clark Road, the train passes by a water treatment plant that's located north of the tracks. We then begin to travel through a highly residential area of Gary's west side; this is the Ambridge Neighborhood.

A typical home in Ambridge Neighborhood (Public domain image)

Ambridge takes its name from the American Bridge Works, a subsidiary of U.S. Steel located on the north bank of the Grand Calumet River. Though Gary was an industrial city founded by U.S. Steel, the Ambridge neighborhood evolved into one of the most exclusive residential areas in all of Northwest Indiana. Housing was chiefly built here during the 1920's for managers at the Gary Works Plant. Skilled craftsmen from the mills were able to live among doctors and lawyers as well as businessmen and supervisors from U.S. Steel. As you may notice from the train, the neighborhood is home to a great number of prairie style and art deco homes. Even through the early 1970's, the neighborhood here was predominantly a Jewish community. Around that time, many of the residents began to move to Miller Beach, being replaced by middle-class African Americans. Famous people from the neighborhood include Nobel laureate Joseph Stiglitz, who grew up in a brick bungalow near the river on Arthur Street.

A view of the tracks in Ambridge Neighborhood (Public domain image)

The Ambridge Neighborhood is traversed by the South Shore Line, however, there are no actual stops directly in the neighborhood. A flag stop was located at Bridge Street from 1920 until 1994. Between approximately Milepost 60.8 and Milepost 59.1, our train travels down a stone median between 2nd Place and 3rd Avenue.

GARY METRO CENTER STATION
(Milepost 58.8)(41.6046° N, 87.3372° W)

South Shore Line at Gary Metro Center Station (Public domain image)

Located just about three miles east of Clark Road, Gary Metro Center Station is the second stop in the city for eastbound trains. It is also known as the Adam Benjamin Metro Center and serves as a multi-modal terminal for local city buses, Greyhound, and other intercity bus systems. It opened in 1984, replacing the previously ground-level Broadway Street South Shore Line Station.

Historical photo of the Broadway Street Station (Courtesy: Sandy Goodrick)

The tracks of the ex-Baltimore & Ohio Railroad (now CSX) and ex-New York Central Railroad (now Norfolk Southern) also lie near the station. Your best views will be when we are on the bridge over Broadway Street; look north and across the Toll Road (I-90). Between the tracks lies the abandoned remains of Gary's Union Station, which was built in 1910.

A historical photo of Gary Union Station (Public domain image)

The station was built in Beaux-Arts style utilizing new cast-in-place concrete methods in which, after pouring, the concrete was scored to resemble stone. Gary Union Station continued to be an active railroad depot until the 1950's. It was featured in a number of movies and television shows. In 1951, when it was still an active station, it was used as a filming location for the Alan Ladd movie called *Appointment with Danger*. In more recent times, the abandoned station was used in the 1996 film *Original Gangstas*, where it served as the hideout for the gang known as the Rebels. Finally, it was used as an example of what could happen to a Chicago building in 30 years without humans providing maintenance and upkeep on *Life After People: The Series*.

You will probably agree that the building is in amazing shape for having not been used in nearly 60 years. However, Indiana Landmarks has placed Gary Union Station on its list of *10 Most Endangered Places in Indiana*.

DOWNTOWN GARY

There are a couple of interesting buildings that can be seen out the south side windows while passing through Downtown Gary.

Two domed buildings can be seen in Gary (Public domain image)

First, look for the two buildings that have a round dome on the roof. Both buildings were constructed of concrete in the Neoclassical Style; one is the Lake County Superior Court, and the other is Gary's City Hall. They both were built in 1927. The area immediately surrounding the buildings is on the National Register of Historic Places.

As the train travels a few blocks to the east, keep looking out the south side windows and you should be able to see a baseball stadium come into view. This is U.S. Steel Yard, which was built in 2001 and currently seats 6,139 fans.

Aerial view of Gary's baseball stadium (Public domain image)

The stadium is home to the Gary South Shore Rail Cats, part of the American Association of Independent Professional Baseball. It has no affiliation with Major League Baseball. The Gary South Shore Rail Cats are in the Central Division, along with the Kansas City T-Bones, Lincoln (Nebraska) Saltdogs, and the Sioux City Explorers. The American Association of Independent Professional Baseball typically recruits college players that were not drafted into Major League Baseball, and former major and minor league players.

Logo for the Gary Southshore Rail Cats (Public domain image)

EMERSON
(Milepost 58.1)(41.6018° N, 87.3225° W)

A little more than one half-mile east of the Gary Metro station, our eastbound South Shore Line train will approach a railroad point known as Emerson. For the past 17.4 miles, we have been operating on a stretch of double track. Emerson marks the first point where eastbound trains first encounter a stretch of single track. Rail traffic east of Gary does not warrant the South Shore to maintain a constant stretch of double track to Michigan City and beyond. Operating with only one track may save money when it comes to maintenance, but it also can create logistical issues when it comes to dispatching trains. When two trains are approaching in opposite directions, one train must enter a railroad siding to enable the other to pass. With two tracks, there are no problems with two trains passing each other.

GOFF JUNCTION
(Milepost 57.5)(41.5977° N, 87.3038° W)

About one half-mile past Emerson, our eastbound train approaches an area on the South Shore known as "Goff". U.S. Highway 12 is on the south side of the rail line; this will pretty much be the case all the way into almost Michigan City. We will pass under an old railroad bridge; it is now abandoned, but once carried a single-tracked spur line belonging to the Indiana Harbor Belt Railroad going into a plant off to the north. Almost immediately after the bridge, a spur line belonging to Canadian National (ex-Elgin, Joliet & Eastern Railroad) crosses the South Shore Line and goes into an industrial park towards the south.

A short distance ahead, our train crosses under the Indiana Toll Road (I-90). Look to the south and you will also be able to see the beginnings of Interstate 65, a freeway that runs 887 miles south to Mobile, Alabama. I-65 passes through cities like Indianapolis, Louisville, Nashville, Birmingham, and Montgomery.

Interstate 65 begins in Gary, Indiana
(Public domain image)

Just after I-90, look to the north and you will see a connector track between the South Shore and Canadian National's ex-EJ&E line. This is used to move freight traffic between the two railroads; this is "Goff Junction".

The old Elgin, Joliet & Eastern Railroad was created in 1889 when several local railroads in Indiana and Illinois merged. For more than a century, the company ran a railroad built line around Chicago. The trackage begins near "Goff" and ends in Waukegan, Illinois, about 30 miles north of Chicago.

An Elgin, Joliet & Eastern switch engine
(Public domain image)

In 2009, the Canadian National bought a majority stake in the EJ&E. The purchase was made so CN could use the belt line for its freight trains instead of using its other more congested lines that head into Chicago's nearby western suburbs. The EJ&E ceased to exist on January 1, 2013 when CN announced the EJ&E would be re-branded as its railroad.

An interesting side note about the EJ&E is that they ran passenger trains between 1889 and 1907. From 1907 until 1909, they actually let passengers ride in cabooses on freight trains before discontinuing all passenger rail services and focusing on their freight business.

GARY'S AETNA NEIGHBORHOOD

Aetna's former downtown area
(Public domain image)

On Gary's east side, beginning around Milepost 56.4, our train travels through the city's Aetna Neighborhood.

Aetna was founded in 1881 as a company town for the Aetna Powder Company, a dynamite and ammunitions maker. The location was chosen in part for its remoteness, in rolling dune and swale country nearly a mile from the small town of Miller. The factory employed about 500 workers, most of who lived in Aetna, although some commuted from nearby towns. Originally the munitions had to be carted to the train station in Miller for shipment, but the arrival of the Wabash Railroad in 1895 gave Aetna its own train station. It was incorporated as a town in 1907.

Unfortunately, the Aetna plant here suffered from frequent violent explosions that caused several fatalities. Newspaper accounts show that a 1912 explosion caused six deaths, and another in 1914 broke windows as far away as Downtown Gary. During World War I, the factory employed as many as 1200 people. However, it closed after the war, and Aetna's population shrank to fewer than 100. By 1928, the area was incorporated into the City of Gary.

Today, just under 5,000 people call Gary's Aetna Neighborhood home. It is dominated by single-family homes. The most recent census report shows that about 83% of the residents are African American.

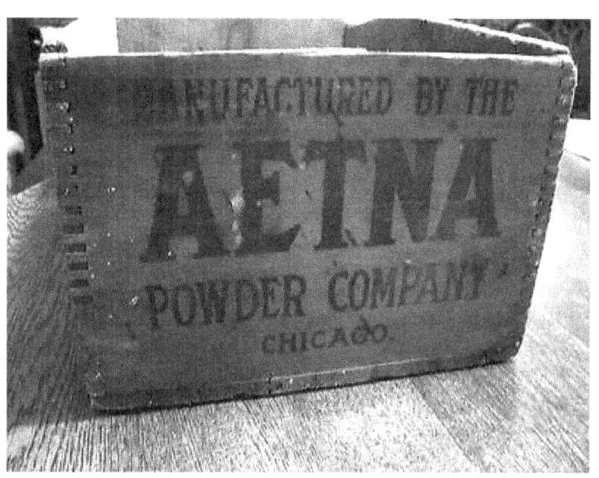

A box of explosives from Aetna
(Public domain image)

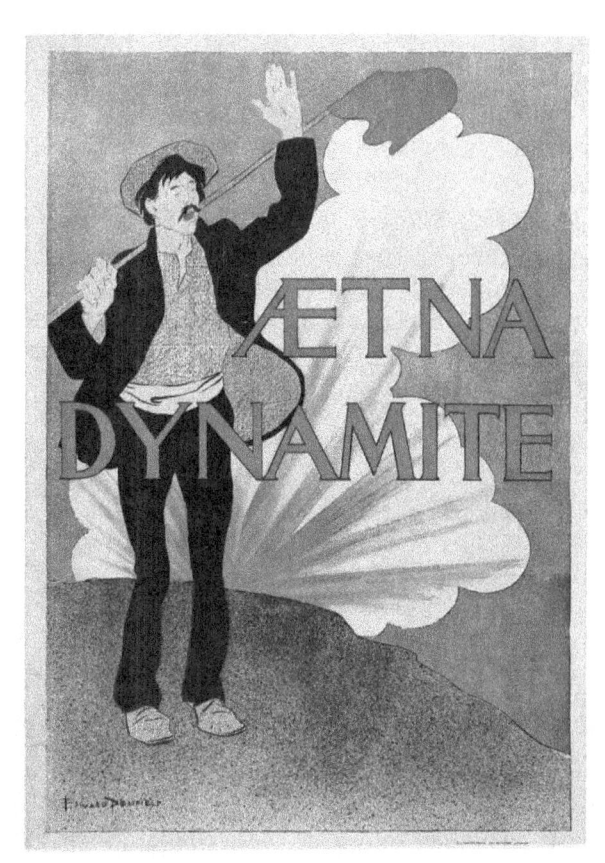

A poster from the Aetna company
(Public domain image)

GARY'S MILLER NEIGHBORHOOD

The final neighborhood in Gary that our eastbound South Shore train passes through is Miller Beach, commonly known as Miller.

Sign near the railroad station in Miller (Public domain image)

First settled in 1851, Miller Beach was at first an independent town. It was served by the Lake Shore and Michigan Southern Railway from its beginnings, and later the B&O Railroad (1874) and the South Shore Line (1908). The person for whom the town was named for is unknown. An early railroad agent recalled the name as possibly coming from a construction engineer named John Miller who lived in the area, and at whose home the early trains would stop for water and wood between LaPorte and Chicago.

Miller was annexed by then-flourishing Gary in 1918, when its town council wanted a lakefront park in its city limits for U.S. Steel millworkers and their families. Being the closest beach resort community to Chicago, Miller has been a popular vacation spot since the early 20th Century. Attractions at one time included a shooting gallery, bath house, miniature railroad, and "night spots" for adults. Today, the former town has just fewer than 10,000 residents, and is known as "The Miller Beach Community".

MILLER STATION
(Milepost 55.0)(41.5978° N, 87.2681° W)

A South Shore Line train at Miller Station (Public domain image)

The third and easternmost station stop on the South Shore Line in Gary is Miller. Located at U.S. Highway 12 and Lake Street, there is a parking lot and small shelter on the south side of the tracks. South Shore Line passenger trains always use the track closest to the highway; the other track is a connector for freight trains between the South Shore and a CSX-owned freight line that we will cross just ahead.

Less than one half-mile after departing the Miller Station, our train crosses a bridge over three railroad tracks. One is the connector track that broke off the South Shore main line just west of Miller Station. The other two tracks are the main line of the former Baltimore & Ohio Railroad. Today, this is part of CSX's Barr Subdivision, which runs from Willow Creek (a neighborhood in Portage, Indiana) west to Blue Island, Illinois. At its east end, it junctions with CSX's Porter Subdivision and Garrett Subdivision; its west end is at the south end of the Blue Island Subdivision, with access to the New Rock Subdivision via trackage rights over the Metra Rock Island District and access to the Indiana Harbor Belt Railroad.

INDIANA DUNES NAT'L LAKESHORE
(Milepost 54.1) (41.6026° N, 87.2530° W)

Welcome to Indiana Dunes Nat'l Lakeshore (Public domain image)

About one half-mile after crossing over the CSX line, our train begins to travel through portions of Indiana Dunes National Lakeshore. It is one of the 410+ units of the National Park Service and is a great location to see wildlife out your train window.

In the just under 36 miles we have traveled so far since leaving Downtown Chicago, you have no doubt noticed all of the heavy industry along the far southern portions of Lake Michigan. Unfortunately to make way for many of these factories, much of the natural landscape was totally destroyed, including sand dunes that towered hundreds of feet high. This began to cause concern for local residents and conservationists more than 100 years ago. In 1916, National Parks Director Stephen Mather held hearings in Chicago on a proposed "Sand Dunes National Park". Due to a number of factors, including our involvement in World War I, protection never quite panned out on the federal level. A decade later, in 1926, the State of Indiana decided to preserve some of the vanishing dune landscapes with the creation of Indiana Dunes State Park. Post-World War II industry in the area picked up even more during the 1950's, leading many to believe that the small amount of remaining natural areas would soon be lost forever to more factories.

It was during this time period that the Save the Dunes Council, including its president Dorothy Buell and activist Hazel Hannell, began their nationwide campaign to buy local land. Their first success was the purchase of 56 acres in Porter County that is now the Cowles Tamarack Bog. Then-Illinois Senator Paul H. Douglas lead the Congressional effort to save the dunes. In late 1966, the bill passed and the Indiana Dunes National Lakeshore became a reality. Four subsequent expansion bills for the park (1976, 1980, 1986, and 1992) have increased the size of the park to more than 15,000 acres. More than two million people visit the Indiana Dunes National Lakeshore every year.

West Beach at Indiana Dunes Nat'l Lakeshore (Public domain image)

Just west of this location is the Miller Woods section of Indiana Dunes National Lakeshore. This area consists of rolling dune and swale, with dune ridges dominated by oak savanna. Miller Woods is a very important part of the National Lakeshore because it is home to the federally endangered Karner Blue butterfly and the federally threatened Pitcher's thistle.

Between here and Michigan City, we will travel through two separate sections of the Indiana Dunes National Lakeshore – they are broken up by the Port of Indiana and Burns Harbor. Imagine what this area would look like today if it was not for those who preserved some of the beautiful sand dunes.

WILSON WEST
(Milepost 54.0)(41.6035° N, 87.2492° W)

A short distance after crossing onto the Indiana Dunes National Lakeshore property, we reach a point on the South Shore known as "Wilson West". For the next 6.5 miles, our rail line will consist of two tracks. Meanwhile, a set of double tracks come into view through the woods towards the north. This is the former New York Central main line, owned today by Norfolk Southern. Amtrak long-distance trains to the east coast, such as the *Capitol Limited* and the *Lake Shore Limited* use this line. Amtrak's all-coach regional *Wolverine Service* trains to Detroit and Pontiac, Michigan also operate over these tracks.

PORTER COUNTY, INDIANA
(Milepost 52.6) (41.6100° N, 87.2225° W)

About 2½ miles east of Miller Station, our train crosses County Line Road. This is the point where our train leaves the City of Gary and Lake County, Indiana, and begins traveling through Porter County, Indiana. It was named after Captain David Porter, who served as a naval officer during the Barbary Wars and the War of 1812.

LONG LAKE
(Milepost 52.0) (41.6127° N, 87.2111° W)

Just across the Lake-Porter County Line, look to the north for a view of Long Lake – part of the Indiana Dunes National Lakeshore. Long Lake is part of a large interdunal wetland area. It was originally eight miles in length, but has been shortened due to development and drainage; its maximum depth is just less than six feet. Amphibians found in and near Long Lake include the tiger salamander, blue-spotted salamander, chorus frog, spring peeper, the American toad, green frog and bullfrog. Some of the reptiles that can be found near Long Lake include the snapping turtle, common musk turtle, painted turtle, common garter snake, racer, Eastern hognose snake, and the six-lined racerunner. There has been an unconfirmed sighting of the rare Eastern Massasauga rattlesnake near Long Lake as well, and the slender glass lizard is found nearby. This area is also a popular stopover for migratory birds. Warblers nesting in nearby forests often forage along the shoreline located a few miles north of the tracks used by our train. Travelers on the train might be able to spot larger birds like the blue heron as we pass by. Many visitors to the Indiana Dunes National Lakeshore enjoy the miles of trails that are located between the Long Lake and West Beach areas in the park.

A blue heron stops over at Long Lake
(Public domain image)

In the 1800's, the ice of Long Lake furnished a livelihood for early inhabitants of Miller Beach, a small town located north of the tracks. Ice was harvested from the lake and shipped to market by rail. The ice also provided a surface for ice skating between Miller and Baillytown. A recreational fishery also flourished on Long Lake in the early 20th Century, when a more diverse selection of fish were present than today, including largemouth bass and perch.

PAUL'S CROSSOVER
(Milepost 51.5)(41.6143° N, 87.2045° W)

Adjacent to Long Lake is a railroad point on the South Shore known as Paul's Crossover. There are switches that allow trains to move between either of the two main tracks here, if needed. In about four miles ahead, the rail line will go back to being a single track.

PORTAGE
(Population: 36,828; Elevation: 636 feet)

Since crossing into Porter County a few miles ago, the train has been traveling through the City of Portage.

After the first railroad was built through this area in the 1850's, Portage residents began to supply milk, livestock, produce, and sand to Chicago buyers. The area maintained its rural flavor for nearly a century, even after interurban trains linked residents to Gary, Hammond, East Chicago, Crown Point, and Valparaiso. During world wars and other boom periods, farmers could supplement their incomes by working at some of the nearby steel mills such as the U.S. Steel Corporation's Gary Works. Portage began to grow in the 1950's when many urban dwellers in Lake County wanted to leave the pollution, crime, and racial tensions behind and move to a more rural area.

By 1959, National Steel ended up opening a mill along Portage's lakefront, and plans were afoot to construct a deep water port nearby. Fear of annexation by other towns finally led to the incorporation of Portage. It now has more than 35,000 residents, including a significant Mexican-American population.

*An aerial view of Portage's lakefront area
(Public domain image)*

A portion of Portage's lakefront went through redevelopment and became part of the Indiana Dunes National Lakeshore in October 2008; this is now called the Portage Lakefront and Riverwalk. Prior to this, the land was used by a steel corporation as settling ponds for industrial byproduct and a sewage treatment facility.

OGDEN DUNES
(Population: 1,110; Elevation: 610 feet)

Near Milepost 51.0, our train will pass through a small section of the Town of Ogden Dunes. Most of the community is located along the lakefront, but our train does cut through the far southern reaches of the city limits here. It was named for multi-millionaire Francis A. Ogden who owned the land here before his death in 1914. During the 1920's, developers planned to create a resort town with a golf course, clubhouse, hotel, and more. As the development lagged, plans were dropped. Despite this, Ogden Dunes was noted for having the largest ski jump in the United States.

International skiing competitions were held on this 30-story high, 500-foot long slide. It was adjustable to both height and length and was operated by the Ogden Dunes Ski Club from 1928 until 1932.

A state historical marker in Ogden Dunes (Public domain image)

PORTAGE / OGDEN DUNES STATION
(Milepost 50.8)(41.6172° N, 87.1869° W)

The tracks at the Portage/Ogden Dunes station (Public domain image)

The first stop for eastbound trains is Porter County is that of Portage/Ogden Dunes. With a parking lot located north of the tracks, this is a comparatively new station, built in 1998-1999 to replace the former flag stop located about 100 feet towards the west. The station serves new residential subdivisions around Portage.

The station has a single ground-level platform north of the tracks. Three small passenger shelters are positioned at the beginning, middle and end of the platform. South Bend bound riders are discharged in the space between inbound and outbound tracks, right over the wooden walkways that connect them to the platform. The station is accessible thanks to recently built ramp structures located on both sides of the track. They are designed to sync up to the first car of the train.

PORT OF INDIANA / BURNS HARBOR
(Milepost 50.2) (41.6188° N, 87.1764° W)

After passing through Ogden Dunes and Portage, our train will cross a bridge over Burns Waterway. We leave the first section of Indiana Dunes National Lakeshore and begin traveling through the Port of Indiana at Burns Harbor. This industrial area was founded in 1965; the primary work done is the manufacturing of steel, as the port is highly dominated by steel mills. The Port of Indiana is divided between the municipalities of Burns Harbor and Portage.

Construction of the Port of Indiana was very controversial, with conservationists fighting to preserve a segment of the Indiana Dunes that occupied the site of the future port. The port and its steel mills were constructed on top of what was once the Central Dunes region and the site of hang-gliding experiments carried out by a crew led by pioneer aviator Octave Chanute. While the Central Dunes was destroyed, it led to the development of the National Lakeshore.

Currently, the Port of Indiana is dominated by three extensive industrial plants: Gary Works Midwest Plant (part of U.S. Steel Corporation), the Burns Harbor works of Arcelor Mittal (this facility was constructed by the Bethlehem Steel Corporation originally), and the Northern Indiana Public Service Bailly coal-fired power plant, which is owned by NiSource.

An aerial view of the Port of Indiana
(Public domain image)

NIPSCO's Bailly Generating Station
(Public domain image)

WILSON EAST
(Milepost 47.5)(41.6206° N, 87.1260° W)

On the eastern side of Port of Indiana, our train passes through a point on the South Shore Line known as Wilson East. This is the end of the 6.5-mile stretch of double track that our eastbound train has been traveling on. Our train line now goes back to being a single track for the next few miles. Meanwhile, almost immediately after returning to one track, our train crosses a bridge over the ex-New York Central Norfolk Southern main line.

BAILLY YARD
(Milepost 46.5)(41.6281° N, 87.1122° W)

East of the Port of Indiana, our train will pass through Bailly Yard, which is used by South Shore freight trains. Most of the railroad traffic is gondola and hopper cars delivering coal to the Northern Indiana Public Service Company (NIPSCO) plant at Baillytown. The power plant and railroad yard were named in honor of Joseph Bailly, a fur trader and pioneer settler of the Indiana Dunes. Citing growing environmental and regulatory burdens, officials announced the plant may shut down in 2018.

DUNE ACRES
(Population: 183; Elevation: 627 feet)
(Milepost 45.1)(41.6366° N, 87.0868° W)

The Dune Acres Clubhouse
(Public domain image)

Near Milepost 45, the train will cross Mineral Springs Road and re-enter the Indiana Dunes National Lakeshore. Located about one mile north of us is the Town of Dune Acres (not visible from the train). It was established in 1923 as an exclusive lakeside resort village. It has remained just that through today, with less than 200 residents. While most Lake Michigan towns battle it out for every tourism dollar they can get, Dune Acres has developed a unique pitch to visitors – stay away!

Residents contend that they take certain very interesting measures, such as staffing a guard shack at the town's lone entrance – on a public, state-funded road – not because they are snobs, elitists or even lepers. It's just that four-square mile Dune Acres wants to "assist lost motorists and keep out big-city problems". They know legally they cannot stop people from entering the town. Maybe think of the guards as greeters, who just happen to stop and question motorists and write down names and license plate numbers if they so choose.

The infamous "guard shack" at Dune Acres (Public domain image)

In case you were wondering, the residents of Dune Acres also don't make it very easy for "outsiders" to access the beaches here either. Since the lakefront is part of the Indiana Dunes National Lakeshore, locals can't completely restrict people from visiting "their" beaches. However, they certainly try their best with parking restrictions that require a permit to park anywhere in the town limits. What is the one and only way to get a parking permit? Become a resident of Dune Acres!

Beginning in 1910, those who lived in Dune Acres even had their own station stop on the South Shore Line that was located where Mineral Springs Road crosses the tracks. It was discontinued in 1994, with residents having to now head to the nearby Dune Park Station.

One of Dune Acres' most famous residents is comedian Jim Gaffigan. Even though he calls New York City home now, Gaffigan grew up in the small lakeshore community. He is known for his stand-up comedy, work in television and film, and for several books he wrote.

Comedian Jim Gaffigan is from Dune Acres (Public domain image)

DUNE PARK STATION
(Milepost 43.7)(41.6449° N, 87.0608° W)

The next station stop for eastbound South Shore Line trains is Dune Park. Dune Park is a comparatively new station, built in 1985 to serve as a regional commuter station and as NICTD's corporate headquarters. The station was designed to replace the South Shore's former nearby station at Tremont, Indiana, a location that was becoming depopulated with the expansion of the nearby Indiana Dunes National Lakeshore. "Dune Park" is so called because the station is physically surrounded by land owned by the Indiana Dunes National Lakeshore. Major units of the National Lakeshore are accessible from the station on U.S. 12 and the Calumet Trail. The station also marks the approximate half-way point between Downtown Chicago and South Bend – we have 43.7 miles to go before reaching the airport.

Dune Park South Shore Line Station (Public domain image)

🚉 There is a siding here at Dune Park that is used by South Shore freight trains; it begins at Dune Park Station / Tremont West (Milepost 43.7) and runs just over one half-mile east to a point known as Tremont East (Milepost 43.0).

TREMONT
(Milepost 43.7)(41.6449° N, 87.0608° W)

The South Shore Line's current NICTD headquarters building and Dune Park station is located adjacent to the former village center of Tremont. It is now just a ghost town.

Historical photo of Tremont in the 1920's (Public domain image)

Tremont was originally established as New City West after City West, a settlement on the nearby shore of Lake Michigan. In the 1830's, City West intended to become a large harbor settlement to rival Chicago. However, after the Panic of 1837, City West was abandoned, becoming a ghost town without a single resident, and subsequently burnt to the ground. Despite the end of its namesake, New City West still maintained the City West Post Office and City West School. About 20 houses were built in the new city after City West collapsed, and a sawmill, cooper shop, and brickyard were established.

In 1853, the City West Post Office was consolidated with the Calumet Post Office, with D. H. Hopkins as postmaster. The Alanson Green Tavern became a popular stop for tourists in the 1850's and '60s; they would dine while their stagecoach drivers exchanged horses. During the same period, New City West served as a major station on the Underground Railroad. However, in 1875 a boiler explosion destroyed the New City West sawmill. The prosperity of the city ended, and it was largely deserted sometime after 1876.

By 1908, New City West became commonly called Tremont due to the establishment of a station by that name on the South Shore Line between Chicago and South Bend. Because of its adjacency to this railway, descriptions of the history of the Dunes often mention Tremont. For example, the Prairie Club beach house built in 1913 by landscape preservationist Jens Jensen and a group of friends was built in Tremont, close to the rail line. In 1929, "scarcely a building of New City West survived"; however, new buildings on the site of the old city led to its repopulation as the summer resort town of Tremont. The purchasing of land for the Indiana Dunes National Lakeshore during the 1960's caused the remaining community to disperse.

KEMIL ROAD
(Milepost 40.7)(41.6634° N, 87.0095° W)

Near Milepost 40.7, our eastbound South Shore Line train crosses Kemil Road. The original Chicago, Lake Shore and South Bend Railway provided a stop here called Keiser. It became a popular jumping off point during the 1920's, being located at the southeast corner of the Indiana Dunes State Park. The stop closed prior to 1977. That year, some local groups encouraged the South Shore to create a flag stop here in order to improve access to the park. The new stop consisted of a gravel platform next to the road. Marketing material encouraged hikers to go one-way between Kemil Road and Dune Park and then take the train back. This quite didn't catch on and the NICTD decided to close the Kemil Road Station in 1994.

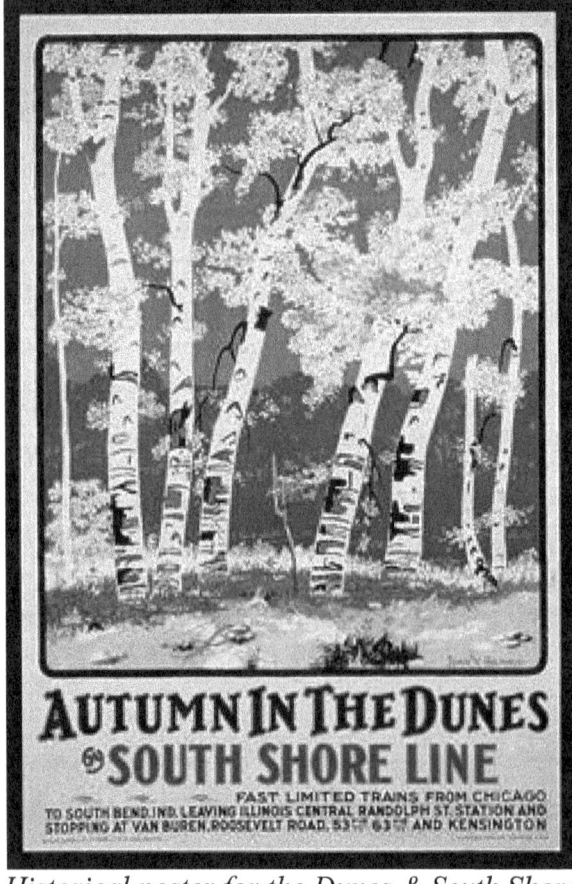

Historical poster for the Dunes & South Shore (Public domain image)

DUNEWOOD TRACE
(Milepost 40.0)(41.6689° N, 86.9966° W)

Northeast of Kemil Road, the train travels near the Dunewood Trace area of Indiana Dunes National Lakeshore. The Dunewood Trace Campground Trail, located south of the tracks and U.S. Highway 12, spans 4.4 miles and connects the Glenwood Dunes hiking trail system to the National Lakeshore's Dunewood Campground to the east. The woods around here are great for spotting wildlife, such as white-tailed deer, red fox, cottontail rabbits, raccoons, and opossums.

Cactus can be seen along Dunewood Trace (Courtesy: National Park Service)

Even though the train will likely be traveling too fast for passengers to see them, areas of the National Lakeshore contain the only cactus found in Indiana. When thinking of Indiana, cacti do not pop directly to mind, right? Interestingly, the eastern prickly pear cactus is native to the lower 48 states of the United States. It is not only a beautiful plant, but it is also edible, and provides food and protection for wildlife. Here at the Indiana Dunes, the conditions are perfect for the prickly pear to thrive in the dry areas and hilltops because, just as the name states, the area is full of sand. For cacti to thrive, they need well-drained sandy soil and lots and lots of sun.

We have mentioned the Indiana Dunes National Lakeshore quite a bit in recent pages – but where is Lake Michigan? It is just more than one mile north of the tracks, but it is not visible from the train. Near the shoreline here, the park contains five Century of Progress Homes that were originally built for the 1933 Chicago World's Fair. Tours of these fully or partially restored homes are available by reservation only one day each October. Visitors have the opportunity to view each of the five homes: the Cypress Log Cabin, the House of Tomorrow, Florida Tropical, Armco Ferro, and the Wieboldt-Rostone House. These homes were built featuring modern appliances, innovative materials, and new construction techniques. These homes, moved later by barge to the shores of Northwest Indiana, are being restored with private funds through a unique partnership with Indiana Landmarks.

A Century of Progress Home
(Public domain image)

BEVERLY SHORES
(Population: 617; Elevation: 620 feet)

The train is now traveling through the Town of Beverly Shores, which began as a planned resort community. The Frederick H. Bartlett Company, at that time one of Chicago's largest real-estate developers, bought 3,600 acres here in 1927, and plotted thousands of home sites. The ultimate goal was to have a city with a similar atmosphere to that of Atlantic City, New Jersey. The development was named after Frederick Bartlett's daughter, Beverly. Things didn't go quite as planned as a result of the Great Depression and Stock Market Crash of 1929. Plans were scaled back, but continued to take shape never-the-less. To lure buyers, Robert Bartlett, who purchased the venture from his father's company in 1933, built roads, a school, a championship golf course, a botanical garden, a riding academy, and even a Florentine revival hotel. Robert Bartlett was also the one behind bringing the World's Fair Homes to Beverly Shores. Potential buyers were brought out to the community on special charter South Shore Line trains from Chicago. Bartlett's promotional efforts met with success, and both vacation homes and year-round residences appeared amidst the dune during the 1930's and 1940's. When Robert Bartlett withdrew from Beverly Shores in 1947, the community was forced to incorporate in order to provide services for its residents.

Historic post card of Beverly Shores Hotel
(Public domain image)

Today, Beverly Shores has just over 600 residents. Some of the locals call it an "island community" because it is surrounded on three sides by the Indiana Dunes National Lakeshore land and on the other side by Lake Michigan.

BEVERLY SHORES STATION
(Milepost 39.3)(41.6730° N, 86.9852° W)

Beverly Shores Station, as seen in 1964
(Public domain image)

The next station stop for eastbound South Shore Line trains is Beverly Shores; this is a real treat for those who enjoy architecture. When Samuel Insull acquired the company in 1925, he instructed his staff architect, Arthur U. Gerber, to design several new stations. Gerber decided to build these stations in either Prairie or Spanish style. Several of these buildings still exist today, including the Spanish-style 1929 South Shore depot here at Beverly Shores, complete with stucco walls and a red tile roof.

Current view of the Beverly Shores station
(Public domain image)

Local historians say the famous neon "Beverly Shores" sign on the roof was added sometime after initial construction, likely in the 1940's. Today, the restored train depot also houses a museum displaying historic photographs and memorabilia, and a gallery featuring rotating exhibits of local art.

TAMARACK SIDING
(Milepost 38.2) (41.6823° N, 86.9644° W)

On the far eastern side of Beverly Shores is a railroad siding on the South Shore Line that runs between Tamarack West (Milepost 38.6) and Tamarack East (Milepost 37.9). This siding allows two passenger trains heading in opposite direction on a single track to pass each another.

PINES
(Population: 708; Elevation: 627 feet)
(Milepost 38.2) (41.6823° N, 86.9644° W)

Welcome to the Town of Pines
(Public domain image)

The eastern half of Tamarack Siding is in the Town of Pines. Tucked between Beverly Shores and Michigan City, this community has just 800 residents in 333 homes; it is very much a bedroom community for workers in Gary-area steel mills and related industries. The only industry actually in Pines is a tanker company and cement block plant.

1950'S ROADSIDE MOTELS

While passing through the Town of Pines, keep your eyes out on the southeast side of the tracks. You will be able to see the back side of two popular roadside motels – The Blackhawk and Al & Sally's. Both took advantage of the heavy traffic that operated on U.S. Highway 12 before the interstate highways opened in the 1960's. These roadside motels may remind you of a time when life was a little slower and there was not a chain motel at almost every interstate exit. Both hotels have just about 15 units each. Regardless of their age, both motels still fill up quickly, even today, with weekend travelers who are looking to explore Indiana Dunes National Lakeshore, but stay away from I-94.

Post card from Al & Sally's Motel
(Public domain image)

Neon sign for Al & Sally's Motel
(Public domain image)

A sign for the Blackhawk Motel
(Public domain image)

A view inside the motel rooms
(Public domain image)

LAPORTE COUNTY, INDIANA
(Milepost 36.1) (41.6989° N, 86.9325° W)

△ Northeast of the Town of Pines, the train crosses U.S. Highway 12. We have paralleled the north side of this highway for the past 22 miles since leaving Downtown Gary. This is also the point our eastbound train leaves Porter County and begins traveling through LaPorte County, Indiana. LaPorte is French for "the door" or "the port". French travelers and explorers named the area after discovering a natural opening in the dense forests that existed in the region, providing a gateway to lands further west. The county seat is La Porte, but the largest city is Michigan City – which the train begins traveling through at the county line.

MICHIGAN CITY
(Population: 31,150; Elevation: 627 feet)

From Milepost 36.1 to Milepost 29.5, the train travels through portions of Michigan City, Indiana. The community is located about halfway between Chicago (50 miles to the east) and South Bend (40 miles to the west). The city is noted for both its proximity to the Indiana Dunes National Lakeshore and for bordering Lake Michigan. Due to this, Michigan City receives a fair amount of tourism during the summer months.

Michigan City's lighthouse
(Public domain image)

Sited on Lake Michigan at the mouth of Trail Creek in the sand dune region, Michigan City was surveyed as early as 1828 with an eye to developing a commercial harbor and city as well as a road inland to transport supplies to homesteaders in Central Indiana. Michigan City's beginnings date to 1830, when the land for the city was first purchased by Isaac Elston, a real estate speculator. He paid about $200 total for 160 acres of land. The city was incorporated six years later, at which point it had 1,500 residents, along with a newspaper, a church, a commercial district, and ten hotels.

A historic post card from Michigan City
(Public domain image)

▲ Today, the far eastern edge of Indiana Dunes National Lakeshore is located here in Michigan City; the park lands are located north of our train line. Nearby park features include Mount Baldy, which is a 126-foot-tall sand dune. It is called a "wandering dune", as it shifts every year. In recent years, park officials began planting natural grasses and re-routing hiking trails to slow the process. On a clear day, visitors are able to see Downtown Chicago's skyline from the top of Mount Baldy.

During Summer 2013, unexpected sinkholes, later called anomalies, began appearing in the sand, one of which swallowed a small child. It took three hours for the boy to be rescued from the 11-foot pit. After a few years of research and study, scientists concluded in 2016 that such sinkholes were caused by the burial of black oak trees that eventually decayed, leaving a "dune decomposition chimney". When this rail route guidebook was published in Summer 2017, Mount Baldy remained closed to visitors except with very limited ranger tours.

NPS Ranger J.P. Anderson at Mount Baldy
(Photo by Robert & Kandace Tabern)

In 2012, the Dunes National Park Association was established as a nonprofit organization dedicated to supporting the Indiana Dunes National Lakeshore.

POWER SIDING
(Milepost 35.6) (41.7057° N, 86.9259° W)

Just after crossing the Porter-LaPorte County Line, the train passes by the start of Power Siding in Michigan City. It runs between Power West (Milepost 36.0) and Power East (Milepost 35.2). The siding and extra tracks are primarily used by freight rail cars supplying coal to Michigan City's power plant. Much of the coal is delivered in hopper cars from mines located down in Central and Southern Illinois.

Michigan City's Generating Station
(Public domain image)

The power plant can be seen north of the tracks. Many passengers may mistake this for being a nuclear plant, but it is actually coal and natural gas fired. There are no nuclear power plants in the State of Indiana. It is operated by Northern Indiana Public Service Company (NIPSCO) and owned by NiSource.

Where the power plant now stands, was the site of a 200-foot-tall sand dune known as "Hoosier Slide" (photo on Page 77). In the mid-1800's, the dune had trees and berries; cows even grazed there. As the trees were cut and used, the dune became bare, probably 1870. Many weddings and picnics were held here. Between 1890 and 1920, the sand was removed for glassmaking in Muncie and Kokomo, and also for landfill in Chicago's Jackson Park.

HISTORIC SOUTH SHORE LINE CARS

An old South Shore Line passenger car that is need of repair
(Photo by Robert & Kandace Tabern)

Rail enthusiasts will only have one chance along the route today between Chicago and South Bend to spot some historic South Shore Line passenger railroad equipment. On the far west side of Michigan City, just before the train crosses Sheridan Avenue, look for a cluster of buildings on the southeast side of the tracks. If you look carefully, there are some old orange-colored passenger cars tucked amongst the structures here (at least when this route guide was published they were still there). It is believed they are part of a metal scrap yard here; however, that has not been confirmed.

If you are looking to ride some restored South Shore Line passenger rail equipment, you may wish to visit the Illinois Railroad Museum, which is located northwest of Chicago. Another good location for vintage South Shore Line train rides is the Fox River Trolley Museum in South Elgin, Illinois. The National Park Service was hoping to build a museum in the Indiana Dunes National Lakeshore about the South Shore, however funding for such a project has since fallen through. Many of the cars for this project have recently been donated to the East Troy Electric Railroad about 100 miles away in Wisconsin; they are also well worth a visit.

A 1908 post card of the Hoosier Slide
(Public domain image)

MICHIGAN CITY "STREET RUNNING"
(Milepost 35.3) (41.7066° N, 86.9218° W)

Rail enthusiasts might find the next few miles of the South Shore Line to be one of the most interesting parts of the route between Chicago and South Bend. Between Mileposts 35.3 and Mileposts 34.6, the train will "street run" down West 10th Street in Michigan City – sharing the road with vehicles and pedestrians.

South Shore "street running" in Michigan City
(Public domain image)

As mentioned earlier in this route guide, the South Shore used to have a "street running" segment in East Chicago, but it was replaced with the a new routing in 1956.

Across the country, the trend in recent decades has been to replace "street running" segments of railroads with new alignments. The reason behind this is mixing fast-moving trains with cars, trucks, and people created a lot of extra danger. The Northern Indiana Commuter Transportation District is considering proposals that would eliminate the Michigan City street alignment segments; construction on a new right-of-way could begin as early as 2019. Getting the trains off the street would allow speeds to increase to 45mph through the city.

The intersection of 10th Street and Willard Ave. in Michigan City served as a flag stop on the South Shore Line between the 1930's and July 1994. Passengers now just use the 11th Street Station located to the east.

AMTRAK MICHIGAN LINE CROSSING
(Milepost 34.6) (41.7091° N, 86.9093° W)

On the west side of Michigan City, the South Shore Line crosses a single-tracked rail line belonging to Amtrak. This is used for their *Wolverine Service* trains that take passengers between Chicago and Pontiac, Michigan via Detroit – and for their *Blue Water* passenger trains that operate between Chicago and Port Huron, Michigan. The crossing is controlled by Amtrak's dispatch center in Chicago.

Our train line crosses an Amtrak line
(Public domain image)

This rail line was once owned by the Michigan Central Railroad, an affiliate of the New York Central. The Michigan Central was one of the few Michigan railroads with a direct line into Chicago, meaning it did not have to operate cross-lake ferries, as did virtually all other railroads operating in Michigan, such as the Pere Marquette, Pennsylvania, Grand Trunk, and Ann Arbor Railroads. Michigan Central was part owner of the ferry service which operated to the Upper Peninsula as well as cross-river ferry service to Ontario, but these routes did not exist to circumvent Chicago.

A Michigan Central box car loading at a dock (Public domain image)

In 1968, the New York Central merged with its former rival, the Pennsylvania Railroad to form Penn Central. The new company went bankrupt in 1970 and was taken over by the federal government and merged into Conrail in 1976. Conrail saw no use for the train line between Porter, Indiana and Kalamazoo, Michigan; they ended up giving this 98-mile segment of track to Amtrak at that time, including this stretch of track that runs through Michigan City. This is the only rail line actually owned by Amtrak in the Midwest; more typically, Amtrak operates its passenger service over freight railroads though a cooperative agreement. Amtrak does own a lot of its own rail line in the Northeast from Washington, D.C. to New York City.

ABRAHAM LINCOLN FUNERAL TRAIN

Lincoln Funeral Train in Michigan City (Public domain image)

At the same point where the South Shore Line crosses the Amtrak line today, our tracks also crossed over the Monon Railroad. The tracks of the Monon have long been torn out, but this rail line used to connect Michigan City with points to the south, including Monon, Lafayette, and all the way down to the Ohio River near New Albany and Louisville, KY.

On April 21, 1865, a train carrying the coffin of assassinated President Abraham Lincoln left Washington, D.C. on its way to Springfield, Illinois, where he would be buried on May 4th. The train carrying Lincoln's body traveled through 180 cities and seven states on its way to Lincoln's home state of Illinois. Scheduled stops for the special funeral train were printed in local newspapers and thousands turned out trackside to pay their final respects. Between Indianapolis and Michigan City, the train used the Monon Route – crossing the South Shore Line here in Michigan City. On the morning of May 1, 1865, Lincoln's Funeral Train made a stop here in Michigan City under a 35-foot arch that was constructed by local residents with such sayings on it as "the national mourns" and "our guiding star has fallen". The train then proceeded to Chicago and Springfield.

MORE "STREET RUNNING"
(Milepost 34.5) (41.7090° N, 86.9076° W)

South Shore "street running" in Michigan City (Public domain image)

Are you ready for more "street running"? After going through the Amtrak and old Monon crossing, our eastbound train will proceed for more than one mile right down the center of West 11th Street here in Michigan City. This will occur approximately between Milepost 34.5 and Milepost 33.3.

A couple of interesting buildings can be seen on the north side of the train while we are traveling 11th Street here in Michigan City. Just east of Manhattan Street (or Milepost 34.25) you will be able to see a church that belongs to St. Mary, the Immaculate Conception Parish. In 1867, two smaller Catholic parishes primarily made up of German and Irish immigrants to build the new church that recently celebrated its 150th Anniversary. Just to the east stands Marquette Catholic High School. On June 27, 1886, the school's cornerstone was laid and a bell was placed in the tower of the new St. Mary's School at 10th and Buffalo Streets. On November 2, 1886, the 80 students moved into their new classroom, which included a high school department. Enrollment continued to grow from 250 students taught by six sisters to 440 including the high school by 1896. Many of the students remained for only one, two or three years and then left high school to go to work. However, in June 1894 two students completed four years of study, thus becoming the first graduates of St. Mary's High School.

MICHIGAN CITY / 11TH ST. STATION
(Milepost 33.9) (41.7090° N, 86.9076° W)

Michigan City/11th Street Station (Public domain image)

Our South Shore Line train will make a stop here in the Central City Neighborhood of Michigan City. The station is composed of a passenger shelter and a sign on the northwest corner of East 11th Street and Pine Street; boarding and alighting is done from the street itself. The stop is located adjacent to the historic 1927 station of the South Shore. Look for the white two-story building on the north side of the tracks, just west of the new shelter.

South Shore's historic 11th Street Station (Public domain image)

📷 Near Milepost 33.7, look to the south as the train passes another historic church here in Michigan City. This was the First Christian Church; it was built in 1925 and added on to in 1939. In recent years a new religious group has taken over the church – calling it Bride Church.

One of several historic churches in town
(Public domain image)

📷 When the train passes by York Street here in Michigan City (at Milepost 33.6) take a look to either the north or south – and you will see something of yesteryear. Yes, we are talking about a brick street. The bricks are dark red in color and local historians say there were installed in about 1910. So why were bricks used when asphalt was around for more than 20 years at that point? The answer boils down to maintenance costs. Cities that began switching over to asphalt pavement in the 1890's reported having to spend thousands of dollars per year on maintenance costs, while spending virtually nothing on the upkeep of brick streets. This caused many communities, including Michigan City, to switch back to brick paving of streets until better asphalt could be developed. Since these brick streets have been around for almost 110 years at this point – there is little argument that they really do stand the 'test of time'.

York Street crosses the South Shore Line
(Public domain image)

MICHIGAN/HOLLIDAY NEIGHBORHOOD
(Milepost 33.2) (41.7133° N, 86.8818° W)

The South Shore Line in Michigan City
(Public domain image)

🏠 On the eastern side of Michigan City, the train passes through the residential Michigan/Holliday Neighborhood. It got its name from several of the local streets in the area. Our train continues to operate on a single track and even though we are not "street running" here, we do travel parallel to Holliday Street. One point on the South Shore Line with a signal is School Street, at Milepost 33.0. Homes with tree-lined streets can be seen towards the south, while more homes with a few abandoned industrial buildings can be seen towards the north here.

80

MICHIGAN CITY SHOPS / CAROLL AVENUE STATION
(Milepost 32.2) (41.7132° N, 86.8676° W)

*Michigan City's Caroll Avenue Station
(Public domain image)*

At Milepost 32.3, our eastbound train crosses Caroll Avenue and a single-track rail line owned by South Shore Freight. This line begins just northwest of here and proceeds down to La Porte, Stilwell, and Kingsbury; it is only used by freight trains and has no overhead catenary wires to support passenger service.

Just ahead, our train will arrive at the South Shore's Caroll Avenue Station. For reasons of road access and parking, it, rather than the 11th Street Station, is recognized as Michigan City's primary commuter station. Even though the South Shore Line continues on for another 32 miles to South Bend Airport, a vast majority of eastbound trains terminate here at the Caroll Avenue Station. There simply isn't enough passenger demand to run every South Shore Line train all the way from Downtown Chicago to South Bend Airport. Even when trains do run through, train crews may occasionally remove un-needed cars before departing for South Bend and store them in the yards here at Caroll Avenue. This happens particularly on weekday evening eastbound trips.

Another interesting facet of the South Shore's operation here at Carroll Avenue is that this is the railroad's only yard and maintenance shop. Since there are no facilities to clean or service trains at any of the other layover points (such as Chicago Millennium Station, Gary Metro, or South Bend Airport) all trains are scheduled to start and end their day here in Michigan City. This means a weekday morning inbound train to Chicago from South Bend Airport will begin here at Michigan City, head east to South Bend, and then back west to Chicago. Many morning trains to Chicago will just begin here at Caroll Avenue, bypassing South Bend Airport and Hudson Lake due to their low passenger counts.

*South Shore Line train yards at Carroll Ave.
(Public domain image)*

The South Shore Line's facility here also serves as offices for NICTD's passenger service and accounting departments. Additional offices, including the NICTD's Headquarters, are located in the Dune Park Station in Chesterton.

Although now un-related to the NICTD, South Shore Freight also has its shops and offices here adjacent to the Carroll Avenue Station. This is actually a strategic point for the freight side of the operations to have its shops located at the center of its lines. Freight trains can head west to the Chicago area from here, or take one of two lines to the east. We will pass by the freight yards as we leave the station area.

TRAIL CREEK
(Milepost 31.4) (41.7126° N, 86.8572° W)

At the far eastern end of the South Shore Freight yard, our train crosses a bridge over Trail Creek. The stream is 7.3 miles long; it begins at the confluence of the West Branch Trail Creek and the East Branch Trail Creek, and flows into Lake Michigan in Downtown Michigan City.

Trail Creek was called *Myewes-zibiwe* in Potawatomi, meaning "trail creek". It referred to the Native American trail that ran from Chicago along the south shore of Lake Michigan, along Trail Creek, then to Hudson Lake, and finally to the French Fort St. Joseph and the nearby Jesuit mission (now Niles, MI) on the St. Joseph River. The French named it *La Riviere du Chemin* (River of the Trail), and in the 1810's it was referred to as the Road River and Chemin River.

An 1869 drawing of Trail Creek's mouth (Public domain image)

KARWICK ROAD
(Milepost 31.3) (41.7124° N, 86.8552° W)

Just before crossing Trail Creek, our rail line will go down to a single track once again. Ahead is the longest stretch of single track that remains in place on the South Shore Line today. We will not reach another siding for another 12.3 miles. Even though there is not much rail traffic between Carroll Avenue and South Bend Airport, this can be tricky for dispatchers who must hold an eastbound train here in Michigan City if a westbound train is anywhere close to approaching.

The South Shore Line at Karwick Road (Public domain image)

CSX GRAND RAPIDS SUBDIVISION
(Milepost 31.2) (41.7121° N, 86.8523° W)

A short distance east of Karwick Road, the South Shore crosses under a single-tracked rail line; this is part of CSX's Grand Rapids Subdivision. Freight trains use this line to head between Porter, Indiana and Grand Rapids, Michigan. This line is also used by Amtrak's *Pere Marquette* passenger train that runs once per day in each direction from Chicago Union Station to Grand Rapids, Michigan. Just past the bridge there will be a connector track that goes off towards the north from our line.

LEAVING MICHIGAN CITY
(Milepost 30.7) (41.7121° N, 86.8523° W)

On the eastern outskirts of Michigan City, the train passes by the city's municipal golf course; look out the south side windows here and you may see golfers hitting the links. The facility features two beautiful 18-hole courses set in a tranquil setting. The North Course, which you're seeing from the train, features executive-style golfing, including 3,531 total yards to play and a challenging par of 60.

Michigan City Municipal Golf Course
(Public domain image)

Meanwhile, out the north side windows, just opposite of the golf course, is a large factory that is currently not in use. It was built for a company called Federal Mogul, a worldwide maker of automobile parts. When in operation, over 100 people were employed here in Michigan City making window wiper blades. Federal Mogul shut down operations in 2012.

DAVIS
(Milepost 29.7) (41.7163° N, 86.8200° W)

Just before crossing out of the city limits, the train crosses under Indiana State Highway 212. There is a point on the South Shore Line just east of here called Davis. There isn't much to see except for a couple of freight spur tracks that go into small factories to the south.

Located just southeast of here is Michigan City Municipal Airport. There is no commercial air service out of here, however just about 7,700 private planes will fly in and out of here in a given year; most are single-engine aircraft.

INTERSTATE 94
(Milepost 29.0) (41.7184° N, 86.8058° W)

South Shore Line passes under I-94
(Public domain image)

Just outside the Michigan City limits, the train crosses underneath Interstate 94. This is a 1,585-mile-long highway that runs between Port Huron, Michigan and Central Montana. Several large cities in the Midwest are located on I-94 including Detroit, Chicago, Milwaukee, Madison, Twin Cities, Fargo, Grand Forks, and Bismarck. It is one of the furthest northern interstate highways in the United States.

AMBLER
(Milepost 28.4) (41.7183° N, 86.7965° W)

After crossing under the freeway, the train will pass through an unincorporated area of LaPorte County known as Ambler. There really isn't much to see here, however passengers will note that after traveling 61 miles from Millennium Station in Downtown Chicago, this is really the first time we are in open "farm country".

OVERVIEW OF INDIANA FARMING

Between Michigan City and South Bend, passengers will see fewer homes as they travel through very rural areas. This is a good spot to explain some of the crops seen while traveling through Northern Indiana.

Rows of field corn can be seen from the train (Public domain image)

Now out of the Chicagoland area, the train will begin to travel through a vast portion of the nation's breadbasket. There are approximately 60,000 farms in Indiana that cover more than 14½ million acres. Farms and forests make up more than 80% of the state's total land area. Most farm acreage today is devoted to grain, mainly corn and soybeans, as seen from the train's windows for the next 25 miles or so.

To understand why so much farming occurs in this area, we have to go back to the Ice Age. The first glacier inched its way into present-day Indiana about 300,000 years ago. The fourth and last glacier melted slowly away about 13,000 years ago. The glaciers flattened the land, while their weight, ice, and melt waters broke apart rock layers which had been developed over great periods of time. These released minerals were added to windblown loess (luss) of fine silt and clay. The result was the rich deposits that became the soils on which Indiana farmers grow their crops today.

Indiana ranks fifth nationally in terms of corn production, but it is the second largest producer of popcorn and tomatoes used for processing. Indiana ranks fourth in terms of soybean production. The state is also well-known for its chicken; more than 41.5 million broiler chickens are sold each year – that means there are six times more chickens than people in Indiana.

Planting in Indiana takes place from mid-April (in far southern parts of the state) to the first week of May (in far northern parts of the state). On average, Indiana farmers plant around four billion dollars' worth of corn. Field corn is not the type of corn that you eat on the cob. It is a special type of corn that has a hard outer shell and is full of starch. The average ear of corn has 800 kernels arranged in 16 rows. One pound of corn contains approximately 1,300 kernels.

So where does it all go? About 20% of corn grown in Indiana is exported to international markets, including Japan, Mexico, and Korea, every year. The Ohio River plays an important role in the exporting of corn grown in Indiana. Corn can be loaded on large, flat barges and shipped via the Ohio and Mississippi Rivers. This is less expensive than if it was hauled by truck or train. More than 46% of Indiana corn is used for ethanol fuel production. A smaller amount is processed into other products like corn starch, cooking oils, and sweeteners. Finally, about 19% of corn grown is used for animal feed, especially in dairy areas.

Indiana is a large producer of corn (Public domain image)

Here in LaPorte County, Indiana about 119,000 acres of corn was harvested by local farmers in 2016. That ranks in the top ten of all Indiana counties in terms of corn production. So just how much corn is growing out your train window? Well, if a typical acre has 30,000 plants on it – you're talking more than three billion individual corn plants, just in the county.

Rows of soybeans can be seen from the train (Public domain image)

Besides corn, another crop that is common along the route of our train in Indiana is soybeans. Indiana typically ranks fourth in terms of soybean production, just behind Illinois, Iowa, and Minnesota. Farmers plant soybeans in the late spring. During the summer, each soybean plant can produce (on average) 30-50 pods, which contain three pea-sized beans each. When soybean plants ripen in the fall, they dry out, change color from green to brown, and lose their leaves. Before the ripe soybean pods fall off the plant, farmers harvest them using a combine. The combine separates the soybean from the rest of the plant. After they are harvested, soybeans are processed. They are cleaned, cracked, de-hulled, and separated into soybean oil and soybean meal.

Soybeans were introduced to North America in 1765 by a Georgia farmer. In 1804, sailors on a Yankee clipper ship leaving China brought soybeans with them to the United States, though for a very different reason than one might imagine. They loaded the ship with soybeans as inexpensive ballast. Upon arrival in the United States, they dumped the soybeans to make room for cargo. In the early 1900's, studies showed that soybeans were a good source of protein and oil, and their popularity began to expand.

A closer look at Indiana soybeans growing (Public domain image)

The vast majority of U.S. soybeans are eaten by farm animals. The same is true here in Indiana. The state's livestock – including pigs, poultry, beef, and dairy cows are the number one consumer of the state's soybeans.

In the fruits and vegetables category, Indiana takes the fifth spot for cantaloupe production, sixth for watermelon, and 12th for blueberries.

So what are some of the characteristics of a typical Indiana farm? The average size of a farm here in LaPorte County is right around 312 acres. Most farm acreage is devoted to grain – mostly corn and soybeans. Some farms produce specialty crops and livestock, including alfalfa, canola, nursery products, emus, and fish. Many farming operations also support recreational activities such as hunting and fishing.

A typical Indiana grain farm
(Public domain image)

There have been some significant changes in how Indiana farms operate over the past few decades. In 1950, there were 174,000 farm operators in the state; today that number has fallen to just around 62,000. During the same time period, the average farm size has more than doubled as sophisticated technology has made aspects less labor-intensive.

During the 1950's and 1960's, the farm was usually worked by the entire family. Everyone had chores. A typical Indiana farm included a large barn which housed hay and straw bales in the upper level, a milking parlor for ten to thirty dairy cows, three or four separate holding pens, equipment room for pails, pitch forks, storage for feed, and a milk house to cool the milk cans. Other sheds housed beef cattle, hogs, and occasionally sheep. There was a chicken coup or two. Larger sheds were for farm tractors, wagons, combines, and other field equipment. The farms included cribs to store grain, an orchard, and gardens. This was a farm where crops were rotated and manure was pitched by hand from the barn and sheds to be spread across the fields as fertilizer.

Today, out our windows of the train, the farms look quite different. There are fewer farms, but they have greater acreage. These larger farms may have a metal bin to store and dry grain, before trucking it to the nearest grain elevator, plus large machine sheds to store the much larger field equipment. One trip across the field can now cover 24 rows instead of four to eight. And, the corn pickers are not lifted and bolted onto smaller tractors, but a huge combine with air conditioning, radio, computer, and GPS on board to guide the field work. The planter counts the seed, amount of fertilizer, and acreage planted. The combine can determine the acreage yield and moisture content. The farmer no longer needs to listen to the radio. He has 24-hour access for up-to-the minute market and weather reports on his computer or new apps. We can travel miles on the train across Indiana without seeing beef or dairy cattle, hogs, or sheep in any pastures. The average age of an Indiana farmer in going up; in fact, here in LaPorte County, it is over 56 years old.

Rural landscapes on the South Shore Line
(Public domain image)

SPRINGFIELD TOWNSHIP
(Milepost 26.8)(41.7179° N, 86.7581° W)

County Road 300W at the South Shore Line
(Public domain image)

For the next few miles, the train travelers through rural unincorporated areas of LaPorte County's Springfield Township. Some of the town services, like a school and fire department are located off County Road N 300W, which the train crosses around Milepost 26.8.

Farther to the east, around Milepost 25.5, the train crosses a bridge over Indiana Route 39. It runs for 180 miles in a north-south direction between the Michigan–Indiana State Line and Martinsville, Indiana.

South Shore Bridge at Indiana Highway 39
(Public domain image)

GALENA RIVER
(Milepost 24.9) (41.7176° N, 86.7205° W)

In Springfield Township, the train crosses a bridge over a small stream called the Galena River. It begins near here and flows northeast for about eight miles. The Galena River will cross the border into Berrien County, Michigan, before it is joined by Spring Creek to form the South Branch of the Gailen River. It ultimately flows into Lake Michigan near New Buffalo, Michigan. Locals say the river was named after Rene Brehant de Galinee, a French missionary and explorer.

LA LUMIERE STATION
(Milepost 24.0) (41.7175° N, 86.7042° W)

La Lumiere was a South Shore Line flag stop located at Wilhelm Road. The station opened prior to 1910 and closed in July 1994 as part of an NICTD service revision. It was named for Edward Lalumier, an executive with Chicago's Armour Meat Packing Company. He acquired 487 acres south of the station in the 1930's. The forest property on which he built an estate included three spring-fed lakes and pine tree groves planted by the Civilian Conservation Corps.

Historical photo of the Lalumier Estate
(Public domain image)

After Lalumier passed away, his family sold off the estate and a Catholic boarding school was established here in 1963. The original board of directors was inspired by the original property owner's name, but changed it to the French spelling, and named the school La Lumiere School, which also translates as "the light". The name for the station on the South Shore also changed its spelling and was used for decades by students to get home during school break periods.

An early billboard for the LaLumiere School (Public domain image)

You may recognize some of the alumni of La Lumiere School. Probably the most famous is John Roberts, who currently serves as the Chief Justice of the United States Supreme Court. He grew up here in Northwest Indiana, and after attending La Lumiere, went on to attend Harvard Law School. Some of the faculty we spoke with at the school remember Roberts as an excellent student and athlete for the school. In 2005, Roberts was nominated by President George W. Bush to be an Associate Justice of the Supreme Court, initially to succeed retiring Justice Sandra Day O'Connor. However, when Chief Justice Rehnquist died before Roberts' confirmation hearings began, Bush instead nominated Roberts to fill the Chief Justice position.

Chief Justice John Roberts (Public domain image)

Other alumni that you may recognize include John P. Hiler, who served as a member of the U.S. House of Representatives for Indiana's 3rd Congressional District from 1981 to 1991, and stand-up comedian Jim Gaffigan.

Even though the train no longer makes a stop at Wilhelm Road, the school continues to operate. It is now co-educational and has just over 200 students. A lot of parents say they like sending their children here because the student-teacher ratio is 8-to-1.

TEE LAKE
(Milepost 23.3) (41.7171° N, 86.6903° W)

Less than one mile east of Wilhelm Road, the train passes near Tee Lake. The small unincorporated community and the body of water for which it was named are both located south of the rail line. Like some of the smaller communities around the area, Tee Lake was founded as a summer retreat for wealthy Chicago businessmen and their families who were looking to escape the city.

*The South Shore Line at Tee Lake in 1947
(Courtesy: Hoosier Valley Railroad Museum)*

SMITH
(Milepost 21.9) (41.7173° N, 86.6687° W)

About ten miles west of Michigan City, the train will pass near the unincorporated community of Smith. Most of the town is north of the track at the Fall Road crossing, and is hard to see because of the trees between the town and the rail line. It is believed the town took the last name of some of its early settlers. Historical records show that John B. Smith started a wagon shop in the area here in 1849, serving those who traveled on the road from LaPorte, Indiana to New Buffalo, Michigan.

SANDHILL CRANES IN INDIANA

Look closely in some of the farm fields near Smith, and you might be able to spot sandhill cranes from the train – especially during their early spring and mid-fall migration periods. The sandhill crane is akin to the heron, only larger. These birds have a seven-foot wingspan and are typically between 31 and 47 inches tall with very long legs.

During the winter months, Sandhill cranes head to slightly warmer climates in areas of Eastern Tennessee, Georgia, Alabama, and Florida. Between late January and early April they are flying over LaPorte County and other areas of Indiana; they will often stop off around this area to feast in the fields of grain. Their ultimate destination is farther north to nest – like Wisconsin, Minnesota, Michigan, and Canada (Southwestern Ontario and Manitoba).

One of the best places to spot sandhill cranes is at the Jasper-Pulaski State Fish and Wildlife Area, which is about 42 miles southwest of here as the crow – egh, sandhill crane – flies. Tens of thousands of sandhill cranes can be spotted here at one time during the spring and fall months. Water is plentiful there and so is their food supply. Since sandhill cranes travel in groups and are creatures of habit – they end up returning to the same area, year after year.

*A sandhill crane in a Northern Indiana field
(Public domain image)*

So why are they out in the farm fields near the train? In the spring, they love to pull up young corn sprouts and nip off the kernels for food. As you can imagine, this sometimes doesn't sit well with farmers because a large flock of cranes can strip a large area that has to be replanted.

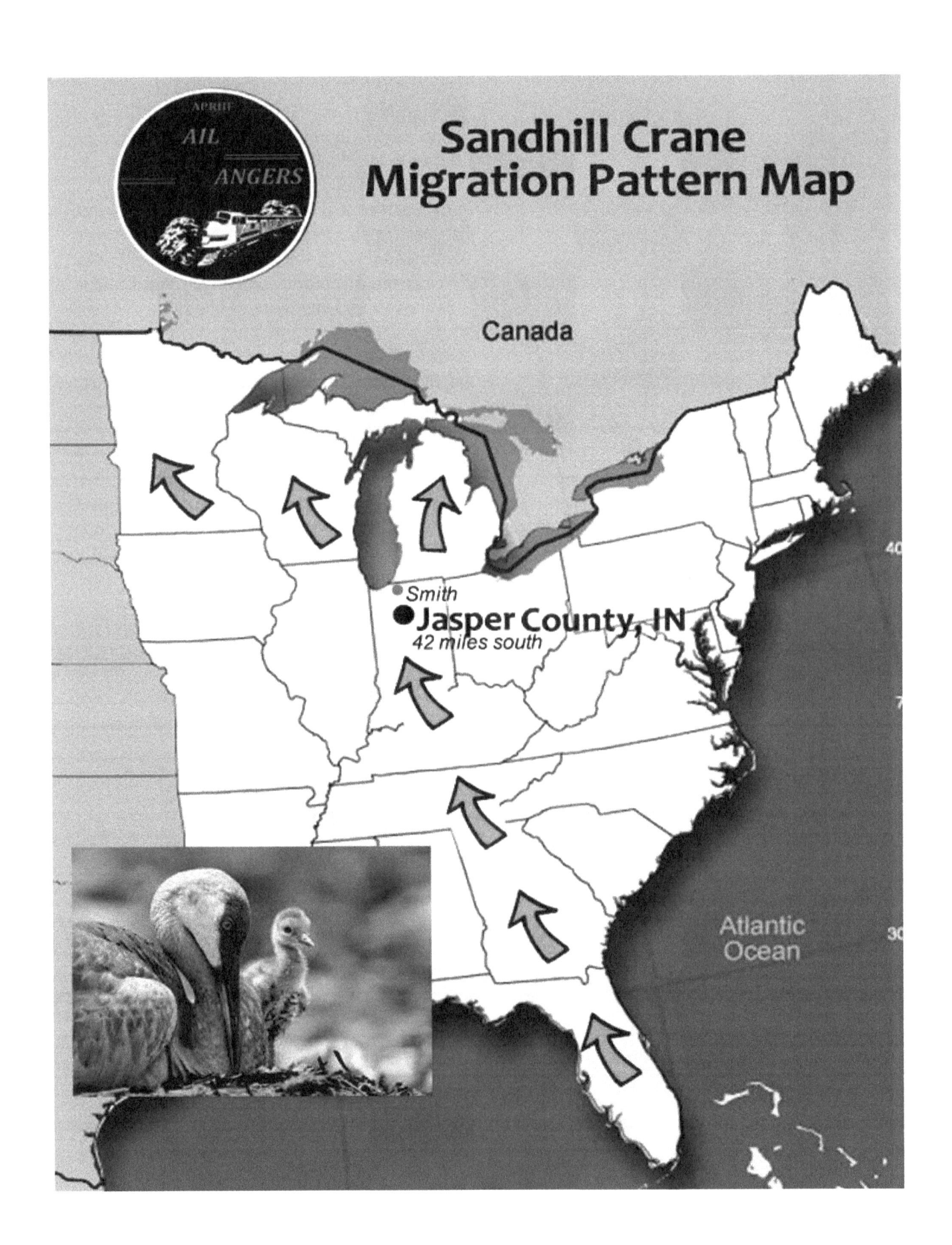

Sandhill Crane Migration Pattern Map

Canada

Smith
● Jasper County, IN
42 miles south

Atlantic Ocean

BIRCHIM WEST
(Milepost 19.1) (41.7168° N, 86.6144° W)

Just under three miles east of Smith, the train will pass by the Birchim Siding. This short stretch of double track between Birchim West (Milepost 19.1) and Birchim East (Milepost 18.5) allows two trains traveling in the opposite direction on single track to pass one another, if needed. Since there is not typically a lot of train traffic between Michigan City and South Bend, sidings are few and far between. This is the first siding since leaving Michigan City; the next one heading east will not be for another nearly eight to nine miles.

INDIANA TOLL ROAD / I-80 & I-90
(Milepost 19.0) (41.7167° N, 86.6100° W)

The South Shore, as seen from the Toll Road (Public domain image)

Just after the Birchim West, the train will pass under the Indiana Toll Road for the final time. You may remember our train line running next to this roadway through portions of East Chicago and Gary about 40 miles west of this point. Here in LaPorte County, the Indiana Toll Road is made up of Interstate Highways 80 and 90; these are two of the longest mega-highways anywhere in the United States. I-80 runs 2,900 miles between San Francisco and the New York City area. However, I-90 takes the top prize; drivers can hit its 3,020-mile length to travel between Boston's Logan International Airport and Downtown Seattle, Washington – literally going from the Atlantic to the Pacific Ocean.

The historic logo for the Indiana Toll Road (Public domain image)

Many drivers, and perhaps train passengers, may not realize that the Indiana Toll Road pre-dates the Interstate Highway system. The Indiana Toll Road was publicly financed and constructed during the early-to-mid 1950's; it opened in stages from east to west in late 1956. The Indiana Toll Road was modeled after the earlier-built Ohio Turnpike and Pennsylvania Turnpike to the east, which it directly connects with. By the time the Federal Aid Highway Act of 1956 was passed to authorizing the building of interstate highways, drivers were able to head from Northwest Indiana to Philadelphia without having to deal with any cross traffic or encounter any stop lights.

Between the Westport barrier toll, near the Illinois State Line, and the Portage barrier at Mile Marker 24, tolls are collected by fixed-amount tolls at exit and entrance ramps. Between the Portage barrier, east to the Eastpoint barrier toll, near the Ohio State Line, it is operated as a closed ticket system, where once receives a ticket upon entering and pays a pre-calculated amount based on distance traveled when exiting.

ROLLING PRAIRIE STATION
(Milepost 18.6) (41.7167° N, 86.6100° W)

South Shore Line trains used to make a flag stop here at N 500E Road; it was known as the Rolling Prairie Station. According to locals, the station opened prior to 1910 and continued in operation through July 5, 1994 when NICTD decided to reduce the number of stations along the route. This move also saw the closure of stations at Ambridge, Kemil Road, Willard Avenue, LaLumiere, and New Carlisle. This was a stop for those who lived in the nearby communities of Birchim and Rolling Prairie.

Historic photo of the South Shore at Birchim (Public domain image)

BIRCHIM & SAUGANY LAKE

The small unincorporated community of Birchim is located just north of the train line here at N 500E Road. The town's name likely honors Abraham Birchem, a pioneer settler of LaPorte County. It's not clear how the town's name changed to its current spelling though.

Some of the homes in Birchim here are situated in a small semi-circle around the south end of Saugany Lake. One interesting fact about the lake is that it's one of only a few lakes in Indiana that has freshwater jellyfish in it. No one really knowns where they came from is the remarkable thing. The private lake, managed by the Saugany Lake Conservation Club, says the freshwater jellyfish are not native – they likely originally came from China. However, they are an indicator species of good water quality – and apparently they like it here.

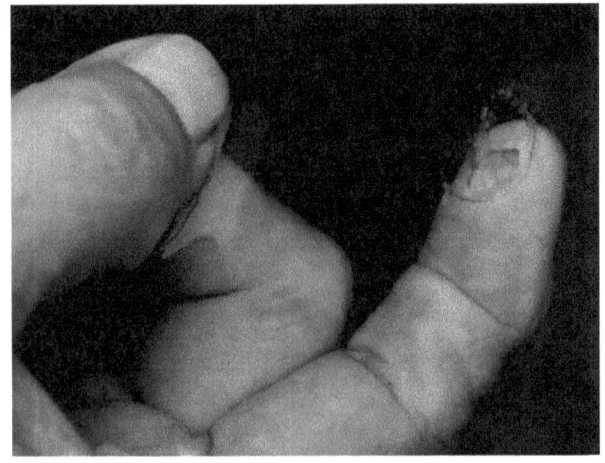

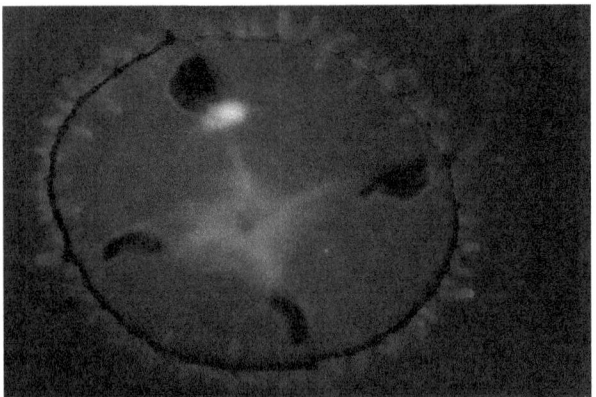

Fresh water jellyfish from Saugany Lake (Courtesy: Northwest Indiana Times)

The jellyfish in Saugany Lake are reported to be dime and quarter-sized, and generally appear on the surface in the greatest numbers between mid-August and mid-October. Some parts of the lake are more than 100 feet deep, so they might lurk closer to the bottom during the rest of the year. Paddlers who sometimes head out on the lake don't have to worry about these critters we're told. Unlike the jellyfish you might think of in the ocean, these freshwater kinds have short stingers that can't even penetrate through human skin.

BIRCHIM EAST
(Milepost 18.5) (41.7167° N, 86.6017° W)

A short distance after passing N 500E Road, the train reaches a point on the South Shore Line known as Birchim East. This is the far eastern end of the train siding we have been passing by. Our train line will now go back to being single-tracked for the next 8.2 miles before reaching Olive West. Once again, train dispatchers must make sure that there are no westbound trains in this stretch of track before allowing our eastbound train to proceed.

HUDSON LAKE
(Milepost 16.9) (41.7128° N, 86.5697° W)

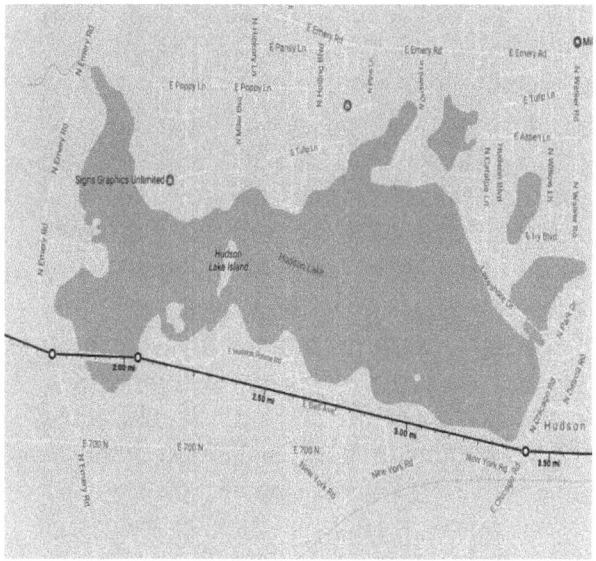

*Map showing Hudson Lake and rail line
(Public domain image)*

Between Milepost 16.9 and Milepost 15.1, the South Shore Line travels near the southern shore of Hudson Lake. This body of water covers an area of 432 acres and has a maximum depth of about 42 feet; the shoreline sits at 763 feet above sea level. The primary tributary to Hudson Lake includes several nearby wetland areas and Saugany Lake, which will sometimes overflow into Hudson Lake.

So how was Hudson Lake formed? Over the past one million years, four huge masses of ice formed in Northern Canada and swept south to bury the northern regions of the United States under thousands of feet of glacial ice. LaPorte County, Indiana was totally covered by ice at least three times. The last glacier – known as "Wisconsin" – crept south over the county 30 to 40 thousand years ago. After reaching Southern Indiana, the glacier then started to melt back north again as the climate warmed. Most of LaPorte County was uncovered 16,000 years ago, at which time the retreating ice mass dropped a tremendous load of rock debris and sand in a broad belt of high ridges we now call the Valparaiso Moraine. Small lakes, like Hudson Lake, were created with-in depressions carved out by glaciers. The melt water from the glacier flowing off the moraine created a gently sloping plain which extends to the Kankakee River. The glacier eventually retreated to Canada, where it completely wasted away about 5,000 years ago.

*Historic post card from Hudson Lake, Indiana
(Public domain image)*

Local historians believe that Hudson Lake was originally called Lac Du Chemin, which means "Lake of the Road", no doubt deriving its' name from the fact that the Sauk Trail passed close to the southern edge of the lake. This was a Native American path running from Rock Island on the Mississippi River to present-day Detroit, Michigan.

Over time, the name of the village located along the shore of the lake has changed, too. It was originally known as Lake Port, but then became Hudson. During the mid-1830's, rich investors from Chicago began buying up lots here in a land speculation deal that called for a new canal to be built between Toledo, Ohio on Lake Erie and New Buffalo, Michigan on Lake Michigan via Hudson Lake, Indiana. When this failed to materialize, most of the town almost shut down overnight. More people began to show interest in Hudson Lake in the late 1800's and early 1900's, as a new summer get-away escape from Chicago and other large Midwestern cities. Of course the South Shore Line provided for easy transportation here for visitors.

Historic photo of the South Shore at Hudson (Public domain image)

HUDSON LAKE STATION
(Milepost 15.1) (41.7094° N, 86.5376° W)

☒ Our eastbound South Shore Line train will make a stop here in Hudson Lake. This is the first stop made in more than 17 miles since leaving Michigan City and the last intermediate station stop before we arrive at South Bend Airport in another 15 miles. The Hudson Lake Station is recognized as one of the very few interurban stations located in a rural region on the United States still left; we are just about halfway between the much larger communities of Michigan City and South Bend. The station is composed of a passenger shelter, a sign, a small concrete pad, and a small parking lot.

South Shore platform at Hudson Lake (Public domain image)

Like most of the interurban railroads of the 20th Century, the Chicago, South Shore and South Bend Railroad was designed to string together farm communities with nearby cities. Most of these interurban railroads have ended this type of service, and the Hudson Lake Station is one of the few such stations that remain. It is currently a flag stop, meaning a customer seeking to board the train here is requested to push a button and activate a flashing strobe light that will catch the attention of the train engineer. Likewise, an eastbound passenger who intends to get off at Hudson Lake must notify the conductor in enough time they can stop the train. If no passengers are getting on or off the train here at Hudson Lake, the train may just breeze through without stopping at all. Only four of the five weekday Chicago to South Bend trains stop at Hudson Lake, with the morning Sunrise Express train skipping the station, and its counterpart the return weekday express train skipping the station. All other trains stop, including all five daily trains on weekends. Hudson Lake is also known for having the shortest platform on the entire South Shore Line, as it is only long enough to spot one train car on. This means that a passenger getting off at Hudson Lake must use the proper coach the conductor tells them to be in.

NORFOLK SOUTHERN RAIL LINE

After leaving Hudson Lake, passengers may notice a double-tracked rail line coming into view about one block to the south. This is the Norfolk Southern's Chicago Line, which runs between Chicago and Cleveland, Ohio.

Norfolk Southern train near Hudson Lake, IN (Public domain image)

This railroad line was constructed in the early 1850's between Chicago and Elkhart, Indiana for the Lake Shore & Michigan Southern Railroad, which was later merged to become part of the New York Central. This was the railroad's main line from Chicago to various points on the east coast. If you were traveling this line in the "Golden Age" of railroading, you might be riding on the famed *20th Century Limited*. It was the New York Central's most famous train, known for its red carpet treatment and first class service. It could complete its 960-mile trip between Grand Central Terminal in New York City and LaSalle Street Station in Chicago in just 16 hours (it even did the run in 15½ hours for a short period after World War II). As more and more passengers turned to driving or flying as their preferred mode of transportation, the New York Central suffered. The railroad merged with its former rival, the Pennsylvania in 1968. That became Conrail in the 1970's, and finally split off to become the Norfolk Southern in the 1990's.

Amtrak took over the Penn Central's passenger rail service in May 1971. This line is still used for Amtrak's *Capitol Limited* train, which runs between Chicago and Washington, D.C., and their *Lake Shore Limited* train, which runs between Chicago and New York City. The best time to spot an Amtrak train on this line is in the early morning hours or mid-evening. We will parallel the Norfolk Southern rail line between here and South Bend.

ST. JOSEPH COUNTY, INDIANA
(Milepost 14.5) (41.7092° N, 86.5249° W)

Just about 3,500 feet east of the Hudson Lake South Shore Line Station, our train will cross County Line Road. It is here that we leave LaPorte County and enter St. Joseph County, Indiana. It is sometimes called "St. Joe County" by locals. The county received its name from the St. Joseph River, which flows through the area on its way to Lake Michigan. With about 267,000 residents, St. Joseph is the fifth largest county in terms of population in Indiana. The county seat and largest city is South Bend, which will also mark the end of our rail line in another 15 miles or so.

EASTERN TIME ZONE
(Milepost 14.5) (41.7092° N, 86.5249° W)

The border between LaPorte County and St. Joseph County marks the point where our eastbound train leaves the Central Time Zone and enters the Eastern Time Zone. This means you will need to set your watch ahead one hour so it will be correct upon reaching South Bend.

Even as late as the 1880's, most towns in the United States had their own local time, generally based on "high noon", or the time when the sun was at its highest point in the sky. As railroads began to shrink the travel time between cities from days or months to mere hours, these local times became a scheduling nightmare. Instead of turning to the federal government to create a system of time zones, the powerful railroad companies took it upon themselves to divide the country into four times. Most Americans quickly embraced these new time zones, since railroads were often their lifeblood and main link with the rest of the world. It was not until 1918 that Congress officially adopted the railroad time zones.

Because of Indiana's geographic location at the center of the Midwest, there have been a lot of heated debates over the years as to whether the state should be on Eastern or Central Time. Residents who live in the eastern portion of the state generally preferred Eastern Time, as they have a connection with communities over the border in Ohio that also observe Eastern Time. Portions of the Cincinnati metropolitan area hang into Indiana, while some people who live in Ohio commute into Fort Wayne, Indiana for work. On the other hand, people who lived in the western portion of the state generally preferred Central Time, as they have a connection with cities across the border in Illinois, which observe Central Time. Many who live in Northwest Indiana and areas near Evansville commute to/from Illinois for work.

Geographically speaking, Indiana should be completely within the Central Time Zone. In fact, the border between Eastern and Central Time should be 82°30' minutes west longitude - or just west of Cleveland. But, the mapping of time zone boundaries isn't exact and residents' feelings have to be taken into consideration. A compromise was reached here in Indiana, with most of the state being assigned Eastern Time, except the far northwest counties around the Chicago area, and far southwest counties near Evansville. Even with that, some counties on the border have switched back and forth.

We are now entering the Eastern Time Zone (Public domain image)

When daylight saving time was proposed, another debate over clocks raged in Indiana. You likely know that daylight saving time is the practice of advancing clocks during summer months by one hour so that evening daylight lasts an hour longer, causing later sunrise times. Those in favor like an extra hour of daylight in the evening and say less electricity is used. Those opposed, particularly farmers, say their day is controlled by the sun and not the clock, and believe daylight saving hurts productivity because they are missing one extra hour of sunlight in the morning. Certain counties chose to observe daylight savings, while others did not. The debate came to an end in 2005, when the Indiana General Assembly voted to implement daylight saving time statewide.

NEW CARLISLE
(Population: 1,861; Elevation: 810 feet)
(Milepost 13.6) (40.7084° N, 86.5080° W)

*Aerial view of New Carlisle, looking east
(Public domain image)*

Just across County Line Road, the train passes through the Town of New Carlisle. Look for the small country cemetery just south of the tracks after the highway crossing here. The area around here was originally known as Bourissa Hills, named after Lazarus Bourissa. He was a Potawatomie graduate of a Baptist mission established near Niles, Michigan, and had been granted this section of land by a treaty that moved most of his tribe members west. The town was laid out in 1835 and re-named New Carlisle, after Richard Risley Carlisle. He came here from the Philadelphia area after purchasing 160 acres of land from Bourissa for the amount of $2,000.

Carlisle apparently wasn't content just being a farmer here in Central Indiana; he went on to become a famous gymnast and acrobat, giving performances at circuses all across America. His first noted appearance was in 1841; he went on to be known professionally as "Professor Risley". As a circus performer, Carlisle is best known for establishing the Risley act, which involves the performer lying on his or her back on a chair and juggling children with the feet. The act has come to refer to juggling anything with the feet while lying on one's back.

*Carlisle and his children, pictured in 1844
(Public domain image)*

*"Professor Risley" during a performance
(Public domain image)*

Carlisle moved to Japan in 1864; he went on to be recognized as the first Western professional acrobat in that country. He eventually returned to the United States and started the Imperial Japanese Troup featuring traditional Japanese acrobats that toured the east coast.

NEW CARLISLE STATION
(Milepost 13.6) (40.7084° N, 86.5080° W)

Even though it was located less than two miles from Hudson Lake, New Carlisle actually had its own station stop on the South Shore for a long period of time. The station, located at the corner of Arch and Zigler Streets, was built in 1908 by the Chicago, South Bend and Northern Indiana Railway, whose line was immediately north of the South Shore Line. Both lines used the station at New Carlisle until the Northern Indiana Railway abandoned its Michigan City–South Bend line, leaving the South Shore as the sole occupant. The station remained in service until July 5, 1994, when the NICTD decided to reduce the number of stops on its rail line.

Historical photos of the line at New Carlisle (Public domain image)

GAVILON GRAIN ELEVATOR
(Milepost 11.9) (40.7037° N, 86.4745° W)

Trackside grain elevator east of New Carlisle (Public domain image)

If there is any doubt we have left the hustle and bustle of the Chicagoland area, just check out the grain elevator complex located on the south side of the train after leaving New Carlisle. This facility is owned by Gavilon, a commodity management firm based in Omaha.

So how does a grain elevator work? A truck loaded with grain stops on the scale, is weighed, and continues to the work floor. Grain is dumped from the rear of the truck. The wheat falls into the pit where it is moved upward to the cupola along the leg by a continuous belt with flat backed buckets attached. The grain is directed to a bin by the spout, which may be moved among the bins.

The truck is again driven across the scale and weighed a second time to determine how much grain was unloaded. Samples of the grain show the test weight of the wheat, moisture, and content plus foreign material. The farmer is then given a receipt, called a weight or scale ticket, for the number of bushels brought to the elevator. The farmer may immediately sell the grain or pay a grain storage fee and hold the grain until he chooses to sell. All grain elevators function in this manner.

ST. JOSEPH ENERGY CENTER
(Milepost 11.9) (40.7037° N, 86.4745° W)

Construction on the St. Joseph Energy Center, as seen in early 2017
(Courtesy: New Carlisle Gazette)

A new power plant is quickly taking shape in New Carlisle; it can be seen just south of the tracks at Walnut Road. Construction on the 165-acre site began in March 2016 and is expected to continue until at least mid-2018. When completed, the St. Joseph Energy Center will produce electricity by using natural gas to turn turbines. This is one of the most efficient ways to produce electricity because the plant takes the exhaust from the turbines, much like you have on an airplane, and reuses the heat in a boiler, that turns a second turbine called a steam turbine. The plant here at New Carlisle won't be the first in Indiana fired by natural gas, but it should be among the first dozen or so. Figures released in 2014 indicate that 76.6% of Indiana's electricity is made from coal, while natural gas accounts for just 7.5%.

Artist rendition of what plant will look like
(Courtesy: St. Joseph Energy, LLC)

The power produced at the St. Joseph Energy Center will be sent to the grid and sold on the open market.

TERRE COUPEE
& THE BLACK HAWK WAR OF 1832
(Milepost 11.9) (40.7037° N, 86.4745° W)

The cluster of homes that you see near the grain elevator are part of an unincorporated community called Terre Coupee, part of Olive Township. The community was first settled in 1828, largely by Quakers. When some of the first permanent settlers arrived here, Northern Indiana was still home of the Potawatomi, and to the north in Michigan, the Ottawa were still numerous and powerful. Some early journals from those who lived here in Terre Coupee recount the fears of settlers when Black Hawk would lead his tribe along the Sauk Trail that passed through town on his way to Malden, Michigan to receive the government annuities.

An illustration of Black Hawk
(Public domain image)

Local historians say that Terre Coupee was also one of the places where settlers gathered for mutual protection during the Black Hawk War of 1832. The famous Sauk leader, Black Hawk, and his thousands of followers had been expelled from Illinois in 1831, but returned from Iowa carrying seeds for planting. Hostilities began after inexperienced militia attacked an Indian delegation approaching with a white flag. Thereafter, Black Hawk and Indian supporters joined in warfare that resulted in 7,000 American soldiers being mobilized. Attacks on white settlements in the area became a common thing between April and July 1832. Most of Black Hawk's band was killed trying to flee west, however. Black Hawk with his son and the Winnebago Prophet, surrendered at Prairie du Chien, Wisconsin, and were sent to prison until the summer of 1833. In that year, the Potawatomi ceded the last of their lands in Illinois and Indiana, promoting the first real development of the area.

I/N TEK STEEL PLANT
(Milepost 11.3) (40.7022° N, 86.4635° W)

A short distance east of the new power plant and Terre Coupee, a large factory that can be seen south of the Norfolk Southern tracks. It is owned by I/N Tek, a cooperative venture between Nippon Steel and ArcelorMittal (successor to Inland Steel). More than 500 workers are employed here at the finishing facilities, which make four different types of coil that is marketed to automotive and appliance businesses. Steel mills at Indiana Harbor and Burns Harbor produce all the raw material for the plant, which is shipped in by train daily. They can crank out about two million tons of cold-rolled and coasted steel products per year here.

A train picks up the finished product here
(Public domain image)

Much of the steel that is processed in Northwest Indiana actually originates as iron ore from parts of Northern Minnesota and Michigan's Upper Peninsula. Using explosives there, a very hard rock called Taconite is blasted from the ground into small pieces. At the processing plant, the taconite is crushed into pieces the size of a marble. The rock is mixed with water and ground until it is fine as powder. The iron ore is separated from the taconite using magnets. The remaining rock is waste material; the taconite powder with the iron is called concentrate. This concentrate is rolled with clay inside large rotating cylinders, which causes the powder to roll into marble-sized balls. These balls are then dried and heated until they are white hot. The balls become hard as they cool; the finished product is taconite pellets. These are shipped by barge or rail to steel mills, like the ones around Gary, where they are melted down into steel.

Freshly made taconite pellets emerge (Public domain image)

Iron ore pellets made in Reynolds, Indiana (Public domain image)

OLIVE
(Milepost 10.4) (40.7003° N, 86.4474° W)

About three miles east of New Carlisle, we reach a point on the South Shore known as Olive. It is an unincorporated community that took its name from the surrounding township here in St. Joseph County that has about 4,000 residents. Located north of our tracks are two industrial plants. One is owned Unifrax, which makes non-woven papers, felts, and boards for high-temperature insulation for automotive, protective clothing, and a wide range of industrial applications. The other is owned by Five Star Sheets. They are a manufacturer of corrugated paper and are one of the largest independent producers supplying the Midwest packaging industry.

Olive also marks the last siding on the South Shore Line before reaching South Bend Airport. It is only about 3,100-feet-long, and would only allow passing for a passenger train or a shorter freight train.

ZEIGLER
(Milepost 9.6) (41.6985° N, 86.4333° W)

Less than one mile east of Olive, the train passes by the unincorporated community of Zeigler; it is almost entirely located south of the rail line. The town is two blocks by two blocks.

East of here, the train will continue along through several more miles of rural Indiana farmland. Since 2007, there has been a more than 27% increase in the number of farms choosing to grow popcorn here in Indiana. Perhaps some of the product you are seeing from the train is being grown for just that. In fact, in 2012, Indiana farms produced 151 million pounds of shelled popcorn.

One of the famous faces of Indiana popcorn fame was none other than Orville Redenbacher.

Photo of Orville Redenbacher
(Public domain image)

Orville Redenbacher's microwave popcorn
(Public domain image)

Orville was born in 1907 on a farm in Brazil, Indiana, which, as luck would have it, is a great place to grow corn. At just 12 years old, Orville began to grow his own popping corn. It became his passion and his first business, allowing him to save enough money for college. In 1928, Orville earned his Bachelor of Science degree in agriculture from Purdue University. He went on to run a profitable fertilizer company and serve as a Vigo County Farm Bureau extension agent in Terre Haute, and at Princeton Farms in Princeton, Indiana.

Any free time that Orville had was focused on creating and developing a new 'perfect' strain of popping corn. He eventually settled on a hybrid type that was light and fluffy, left hardly any un-popped kernels, and had minimal hulls. Orville ended up going into business with a man named Charlie Bowman. The two called their new hybrid popping corn 'RedBow', but were persuaded to change the name by an advertising agency. The result struck gold – Orville Redenbacher Popcorn. At first, Orville sold the kernels from the back seat of his car. Around 1972, however, Redenbacher began appearing in television commercials as himself, hawking his new popcorn.

Initially bought by Hunt-Wesson Foods in 1976, Orville Redenbacher's popcorn, through a series of business buy-outs, settled under the umbrella of food giant ConAgra. Redenbacher continued to appear in television commercials, sometimes with his grandson, Gary. Orville became very recognizable by his white hair, bow tie, and glasses; he truly became a much beloved pitchman. Consumers were confused as to whether or not he was an actor, so Orville even appeared on television shows to clear up the confusion. In 1989, Redenbacher went with the modern times and launched a line of light microwave popcorn. A few years later, a line of 'Smart Pop' 94% fat free microwave popcorn was created.

So what exactly is Redenbacher's connection to Northwest Indiana? Orville always referred to Valparaiso, a city about 12 miles south of the Dune Park Station on the South Shore, as his "hometown", since this is where he lived while developing what he considered the 'perfect popcorn' kernel. ConAgra Foods closed the Orville Redenbacher Popcorn factory in Valparaiso in June 2000, after 30 years in operation. However, the sister production facility down in Rensselaer remains lucrative.

HISTORIC RAIL BRIDGE ABUTMENT
(Milepost 7.3) (41.6941° N, 86.3948° W)

A historic railroad bridge abutment can be seen just west of Lydick, Indiana
(Public domain image)

Rail enthusiasts might be interested in an old bridge abutment that can be seen south of the South Shore Line and Norfolk Southern tracks, just about six-tenths of a mile west of Lydick (or around Milepost 7.3).

This abutment once supported a bridge on a 36.9-mile-long rail line between South Bend, Indiana and St. Joseph, Michigan. It was built by the Indiana & Lake Michigan Railway Co., and opened to trains on August 4, 1890. Upon completion, operation of the line was assumed by the Terre Haute & Indianapolis Railroad Company. Eventually, the tracks came under ownership of the Michigan Central Railroad, which was under control of New York Central.

In the early 1900's, the Michigan Central ran three passenger trains per day on this rail line between South Bend and St. Joseph. Most of the passenger were not traveling between these two cities, but instead, were heading to Galien, Michigan. It is here they could connect with through trains heading west to Chicagoland or east to the Detroit area. By 1919, service had diminished to just one round trip daily. Regular passenger trains stopped running in the 1920's. Since the New York Central already had a more valuable route between South Bend and Benton Harbor, they filed for abandonment of this rail line in November 1942. The rails and the bridge over the South Shore were removed in 1943, with the metal used for World War II efforts.

A view of the old Michigan Central Bridge over the South Shore Line near Lydick, Indiana
(Courtesy: George Ussher Photo / George Strombeck Collection)

The overhead bridge can be seen in the far left side of this historic South Shore Line photo
(Courtesy: William Middleton)

LYDICK
(Milepost 6.7) (41.6923° N, 86.3802° W)

One of the last unincorporated towns that we pass through on our eastbound journey today is called Lydick. It was founded in the late 1830's and was called Warren Center; this was due to its position at the center of Warren Township, which we are now traveling through. It was renamed Sweet Home in 1885, and in 1902 was renamed again to Lindley. It was renamed once more to Lydick in 1909.

Numerous bogs and wetlands around Lydick (Courtesy: South Bend Tribune)

The area around Lydick, especially north of our rail line, is known for its many wetlands, and even bogs. A bog is a specific type of wetland that accumulates peat, a deposit of dead plant material – often mosses, and in a majority of cases, sphagnum moss. Bogs occur where the water at the ground surface is acidic and low in nutrients. Water flowing out of bogs has a characteristic brown color, which comes from dissolved peat tannis. Some of the bogs around Lydick amazingly contain insect-eating plants. A group called the Shirley Heinze Land Trust recently purchased 176 acres of land close to Lydick in hopes of preserving once such bog. Some of the carnivorous plants include the Spoonleaf sundrew, Round-leaved sundew, Purple pitcher plant, Horned bladderwort, and the Hidden-fruited bladderwort.

The bog around Lydick is not yet open to the public or has any markings indicating its location, however a similar area called Pinhook Bog is sometimes open to visitors to the Indiana Dunes National Lakeshore. It also features similar carnivorous plants.

An Indiana Dunes Ranger in Pinhook Bog (Photo by Robert & Kandace Tabern)

An insect-eating pitcher plant in Pinhook Bog (Photo by Robert & Kandace Tabern)

Just east of Lydick, there are several smaller lakes, leading locals to call this the "Chain O'Lakes" region of Central Indiana. The tracks of the South Shore Line pass between North Chain Lake and South Chain Lake. This is a popular get-a-way spot for people living in South Bend. Golfers may also be spotted south of the train line at the South Bend Country Club. A point on the South Shore Line near here, at Milepost 5.4, is called Fisher.

U.S. HIGHWAY 20 & 31 BYPASS
(Milepost 4.6) (41.6877° N, 86.3407° W)

⚠ About five miles west of the South Bend Airport, the South Shore Line passes under U.S. Highways 20 and 31. Both of these highways passed through Downtown South Bend until a new bypass was built to steer traffic around the west side of the city center. U.S. 20 is known as the longest road in the United States, running 3,365 miles between Newport, Oregon and Boston, Massachusetts. U.S. 31 is 1,280 miles long and takes drivers from Northern Michigan to the Gulf of Mexico in Alabama.

The South Shore & NS rail lines from US 20-31 (Public domain image)

The original routes of U.S. 20 and U.S. 31 are now marked as a "business route" of the same highway.

ARDMORE
(Milepost 4.3) (41.6899° N, 86.3607° W)

🏠 Before crossing into South Bend, the train will pass through unincorporated Ardmore. The town is believed to have gotten its name from Ardmore, Pennsylvania, where some of the early settlers resided in. Residential areas can be seen to the north side of the tracks; this is a pleasant area to live with homes scattered amongst wooded lots.

Located to the south of our rail line and the Norfolk Southern line is a small quarry. Indiana and some of its surrounding states host large deposits of limestone or dolomite bedrock that make excellent crushed stone products. The process for this started 300 million years ago when an inland sea covered most of the Midwest. The sea teemed with billions of microscopic creatures and shell fish. When they died, their calcium-rich carcaases settled into the mud at the bottom. After a while, say 40 to 60 million years later, the sea dried up and the mud and sea creatures fossilized. Eventually, the mud and sea creatures were covered over by the earth. During the most recent Ice Age, huge glaciers slid south over Indiana, exposing areas of ancient bedrock, or at least bringing it close enough to the surface that it could be mined. Stone is tested before mining begins; geologists look at maps, drill cores, analyze rock, and locate promising deposits. A lot of crushed stone is used to make roads. Crushed stone is also mixed with cement, sand, and water to make concrete. Since crushed stone is relatively cheap, but the cost of hauling it is relatively expensive, most of it is used locally.

Aerial view of the small quarry at Ardmore (Public domain image)

One of the most famous quarries is located in Southern Indiana. More than 18,000 tons of stone were taken from the Empire Quarry for the building of the Empire State Building.

SOUTH BEND
(Population: 101,190; Elevation: 799 feet)
(Milepost 3.7) (41.6851° N, 86.3223° W)

About 3.7 miles from the end of the line at the airport, our train crosses over Mayflower Road and enters the city limits of South Bend. This is the largest city in Northern Indiana and home to a lot of interesting history and culture that you will hopefully get to explore.

Rich herds and supplies of deer, wolf, black bear, fox, mink, otter, and muskrat first attracted European-American settlers to the St. Joseph River Valley. In 1820, Pierre Navarre established a trading post of the American Fur Company in the area; Navarre was soon joined by fellow agent Alexis Coquillard of Detroit.

South Bend was originally connected to the rest of Indiana by the Michigan Road. It ran from Madison on the Ohio River in Southeast Indiana to Michigan City on Lake Michigan in the northwest via Indianapolis, the state's centrally located capital. In 1826, Governor James B. Ray made a treaty with the regional Potawatomi people for a sliver of land 100 feet wide. The road was built during the 1830's and 1840's, and became a major route for pioneers who would arrive by the Ohio River and then follow the road to their chosen destination.

South Bend was not envisioned as a stop on the highway, but the more direct, northwestern route to Michigan City was hampered by the swampy floodplain of the Kankakee River, forcing engineers to shift the proposed road to the east. Alexis Coquillard laid out the town in 1831 and it came to be known as South Bend, a reference to the natural curve of the Saint Joseph River. Owning a great amount of land, Coquillard was active in promoting the development of the community and donated parcels for schools and churches while also investing in business ventures such as flour and saw mills.

An early illustration of South Bend (Public domain image)

Although the state legislature chartered a railroad in 1838 to run from Indiana's eastern boundary to Michigan City via South Bend, nothing immediately came of this effort. By 1850, the Michigan Southern Railroad had built a line from Toledo to Hillsdale only a few miles distant from the northeast border of Indiana. Michigan Southern hoped to proceed to Chicago but needed to build through Indiana to do so and thus the Northern Indiana Railroad was formed to continue the work. The two companies immediately consolidated to form the Michigan Southern and Northern Indiana Railway (MS&NI) and construction began towards the southwest. The railroad finally arrived in South Bend on a fall evening in October 1851. Headed by the steam locomotive the "John Stryker," the citizens greeted the new era with great fanfare including bonfires and cannon shots. Years later, the MS&NI consolidated with the Lake Shore Railroad providing a connection to Buffalo. At the dawn of the 20th Century, South Bend hosted eight railroads—including the Grand Trunk Western and Michigan Central—providing vital links to the entire country.

Development along the river and man-made canals helped South Bend grow as an industrial center. One of these early businesses was a wagon shop owned by Henry Studebaker; subsequent generations would grow the shop into the famed automobile manufacturer that retained its headquarters in town. Studebaker had its first major growth spurt during the Civil War when the company supplied wagons to the Union Army.

Singer Sewing Company established a factory, as did Oliver Chilled Plow Company, one of the biggest makers of this all important agricultural tool. Across the river in Notre Dame, Indiana, rose the nascent Notre Dame University which was to have a large impact on the future of South Bend.

University of Norte Dame Campus (Public domain image)

GRANDVIEW
(Milepost 3.2) (41.6834° N, 86.3101° W)

Grandview, on the South Shore Line (Public domain image)

A short distance after crossing into South Bend, the train will reach a point on the South Shore known as Grandview. It is named for Grandview Avenue, a street the train crosses at Milepost 3.2. This marks the point where our train leaves the historic South Shore routing.

Up until 1992 when the NICTD re-located the train station to the South Bend Airport, South Shore Line trains would continue going straight at Grandview Avenue (instead of taking the turn to the left). About 1.2 miles ahead is the Amtrak station on Washington Street that the South Shore Line shared with the long-distance carrier for about 20 years; locals call this the Bendix Station. Four Amtrak trains still stop here every day, including the *Capitol Limited* and the *Lake Shore Limited*. The old abandoned South Shore Line tracks can still be seen here, running between the Norfolk Southern Line and the station.

Prior to the Bendix Station being opened in 1970, both the South Shore continued into Downtown South Bend using "street running", largely down Orange Street and LaSalle Avenues. The South Shore Line ended at a small yard on what today resembles an island between the East Race Canal and the St. Joseph River. An apartment complex on the eastern edge of downtown called 'The Pointe at St. Joseph' occupies the former rail yard of the South Shore. The actual passenger terminal for Downtown South Bend was located near Michigan Street and LaSalle Avenue.

Historical photo – South Bend "street running" (Public domain image)

Prior to 1970, intercity trains used South Bend Union Station located at 326 W. South Street.

We return now to the "new" routing of the South Shore Line that our train will be using for its final few miles. Just after crossing Grandview Avenue, our train will take a curve to the left. This has been the main routing for passenger trains since 1992 to access the airport station, but it's really just a barely upgraded former freight spur line. Speeds on the line are just ten miles per hour, which means it will take a good ten minutes to reach the 'end of the line' from Grandview Avenue.

HONEYWELL AEROSPACE PLANT
(Milepost 2.6) (41.6845° N, 86.2995° W)

The South Shore passes Honeywell Aerospace (Public domain image)

A short distance after making the curve off the former main line, our South Shore Line train passes Honeywell Aerospace's plant (to the south). Workers make brakes and wheels for commercial and military aircraft. That's not an easy job, considering parts made here are used on the F/A-18 Hornet, which can cost upwards of 57 million dollars and flies at a top speed of 1,190 miles per hour. Honeywell also makes the brakes and wheels for the F-35 Join Strike Fighter, which flies at similar speeds and is designed to perform both ground attack and air defense missions.

BENDIX
(Milepost 1.9) (41.6855° N, 86.2933° W)

South Shore Line crosses Bendix Avenue (Public domain image)

Just past the Honeywell Plant, the South Shore tracks cross Bendix Drive. The train will run adjacent to this street, on the east side, for the next mile or so. The homes to the east of the track are part of South Bend's Lincoln Manor Neighborhood. Several old industrial areas and fast food restaurants are located across the road to the west.

The train continues north along Bendix Drive, crossing Lincoln Way near Milepost 1.5. This was the original U.S. Route 20, before it was relocated to the interstate-like bypass that we crossed under on the western outskirts of town. This route is now Business U.S. 20.

North of Lincoln Way, our train parallels a large cement plant to the east. Rail enthusiasts will like the green switcher engine and giant red shovel located on the property near the main entrance. The facility is operated by Kuert Concrete; they even have their own sand and gravel quarry located on the north side of the property here. The city of South Bend has even called on Kuert's expertise for a custom color mix to help beautify the city's crosswalks and turnabouts.

Switcher engine located at Kuert Concrete
(Public domain image)

SOUTH BEND AIRPORT STATION
(Milepost 0.0) (41.7007° N, 86.3111° W)

🅧 In its final one mile stretch, the train will cut back across Bendix Drive and make a turn to the west. On its way into the terminal, the airport's runways can be seen to the north while some small businesses are south. Finally, 90 miles after leaving Chicago, we arrive at the South Shore Line's South Bend Airport Station – the "end of the line" for us and the guidebook.

The station has a ticket office and a waiting room. Because the station is incorporated into the South Bend International Airport building, riders can also take advantage of its extensive lounging areas, shops and a meditation room.

Until around November 2009, most eastbound weekend South Shore Line trains terminated at the South Bend Airport Station. Since then, those trips have been cut in half, creating much larger gaps in service, to improve on-time performance for South Shore trains, which had suffered because the section of the line between Michigan City and South Bend is almost all single-tracked. Thus, if the westbound train got delayed, the eastbound train got delayed even longer because it needed to wait for the westbound train to clear the track.

South Shore Line train at the airport station
(Public domain image)

Although the airport train station has two tracks (with times when two trains are scheduled to be in the station at the same time) none are stored in the station overnight. The first and last trains pretty much deadhead to and from the Carroll Avenue Yard in Michigan City.

A new bi-level South Shore train at the airport
(Public domain image)

We hope you enjoyed your ride on the South Shore Line today between Chicago and South Bend, especially if you had APRHF Rail Rangers' Interpretive Guides on your train. Each onboard educational program that we present is different, so we hope you will come back and ride with us again soon. We also hope this route guidebook enhanced your experience and covered some other interesting stories that we were not able to share with you.

SOUTH SHORE LINE
RAIL RANGERS ROUTE MAP
Cook County, IL

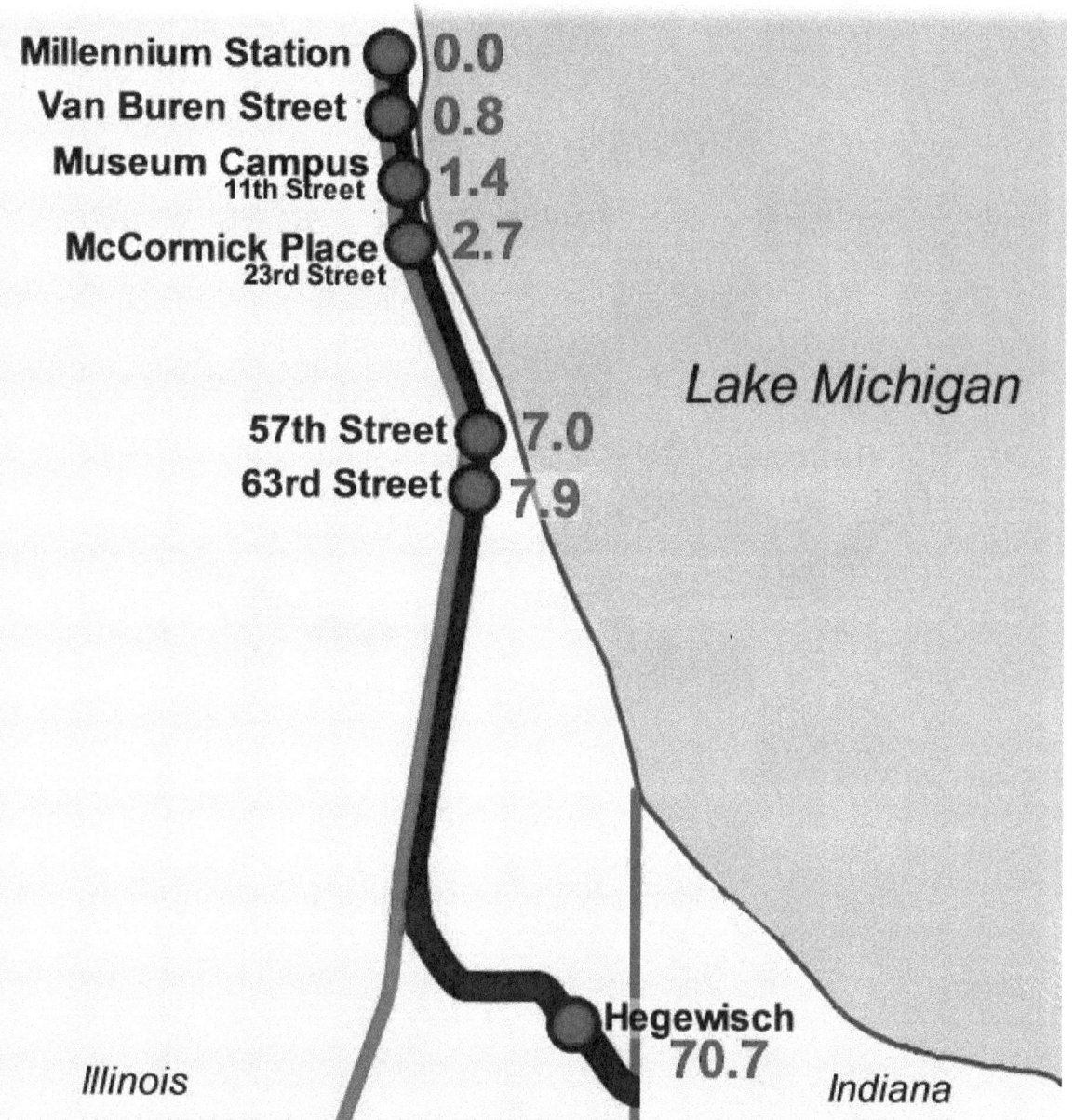

Station	Mile
Millennium Station	0.0
Van Buren Street	0.8
Museum Campus / 11th Street	1.4
McCormick Place / 23rd Street	2.7
57th Street	7.0
63rd Street	7.9
Hegewisch	70.7

SOUTH SHORE LINE
RAIL RANGERS ROUTE MAP
Lake County, IN

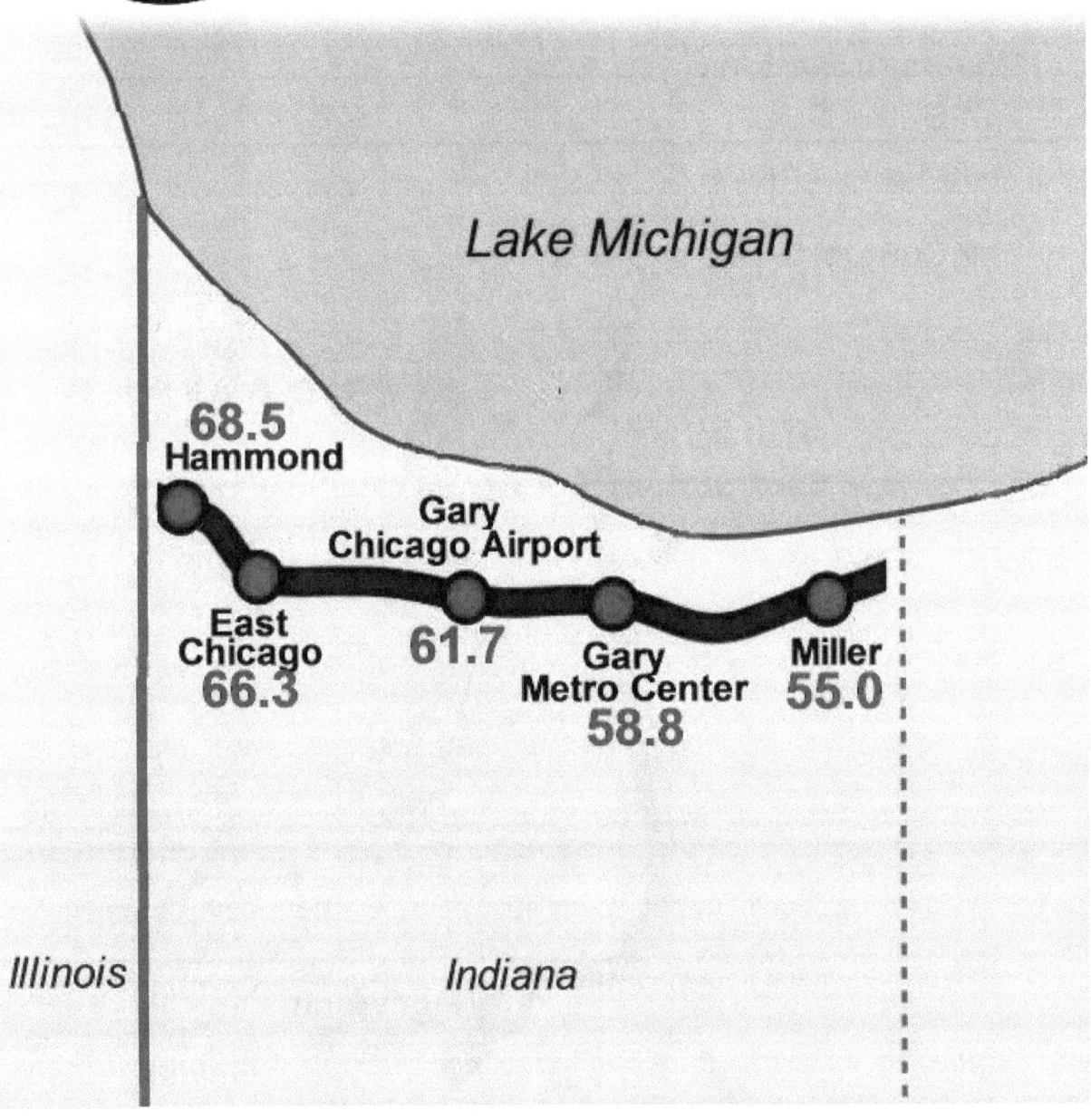

Lake Michigan

- 68.5 Hammond
- East Chicago 66.3
- 61.7
- Gary Chicago Airport
- Gary Metro Center 58.8
- Miller 55.0

Illinois | Indiana

SOUTH SHORE LINE
RAIL RANGERS ROUTE MAP
Porter County, IN

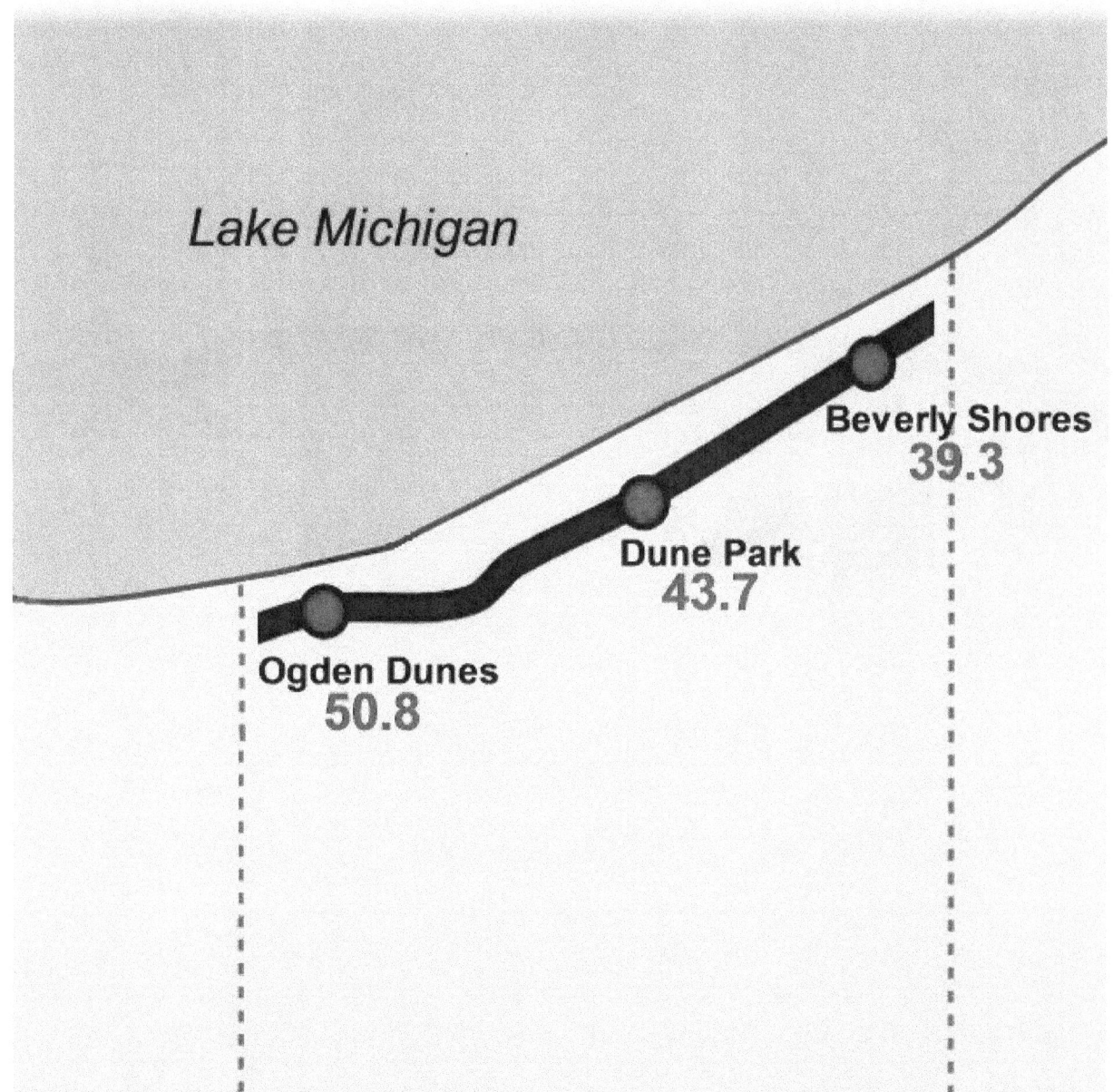

Lake Michigan

Beverly Shores
39.3

Dune Park
43.7

Ogden Dunes
50.8

RAIL RANGERS ROUTE MAP
LaPorte County, IN

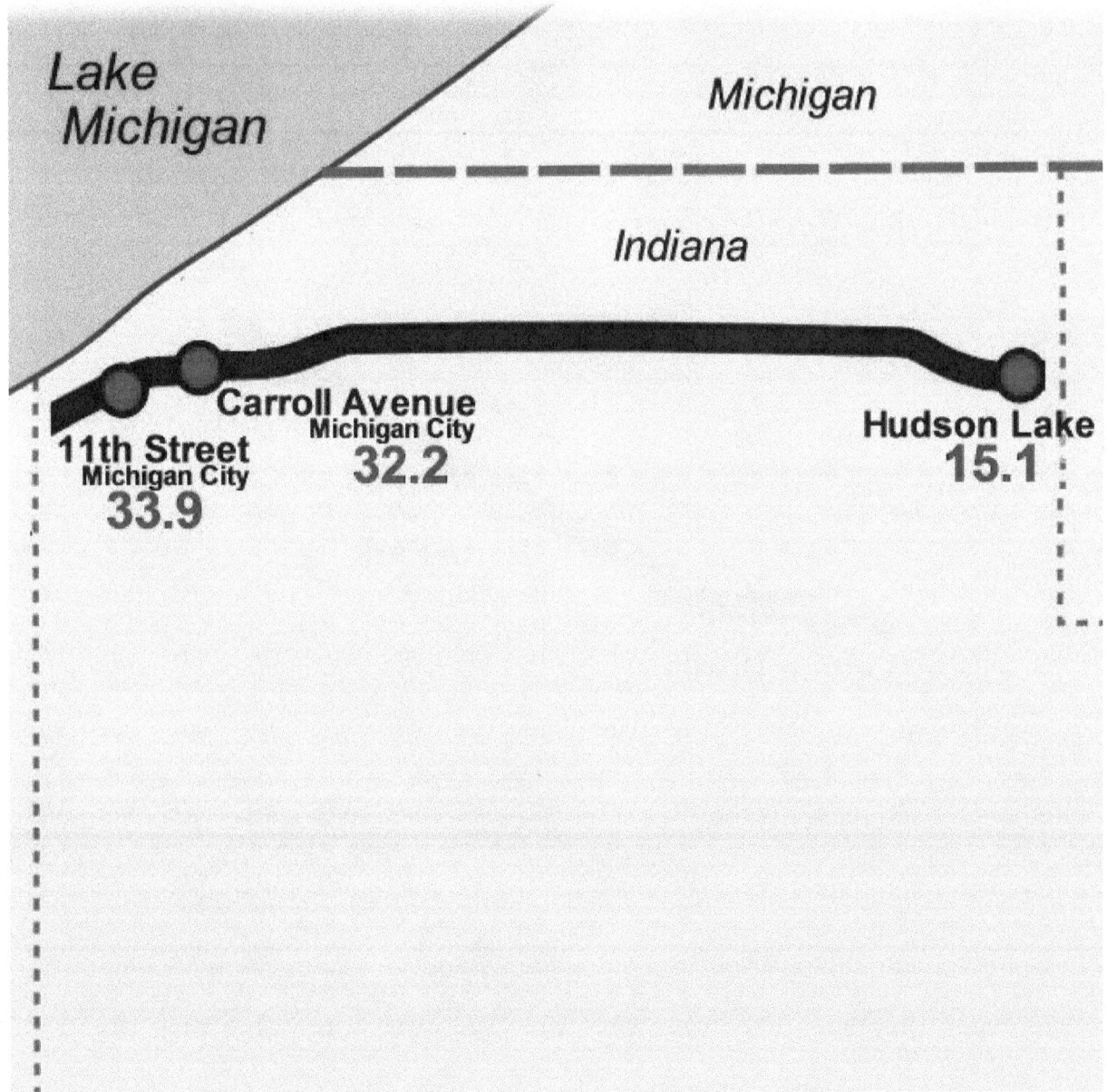

Lake Michigan

Michigan

Indiana

11th Street Michigan City **33.9**

Carroll Avenue Michigan City **32.2**

Hudson Lake 15.1

RAIL RANGERS ROUTE MAP
St. Joseph County, IN

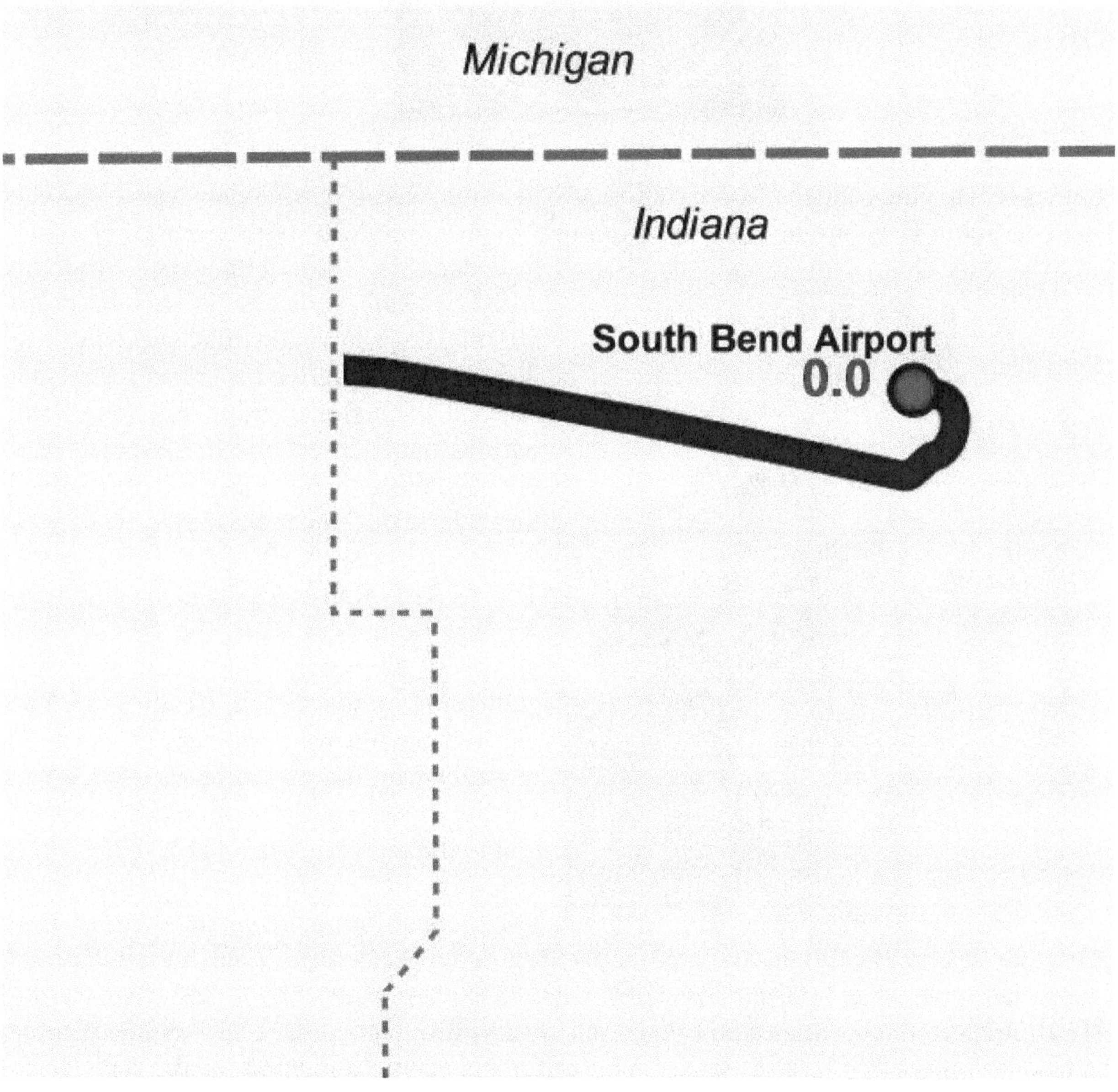

Michigan

Indiana

South Bend Airport
0.0

ABOUT THE APRHF RAIL RANGERS

This railroad route guide and the live narration provided for passengers on select trains between Chicago and South Bend are brought to you in part by the American Passenger Rail Heritage Foundation's Rail Rangers program. APRHF Rail Rangers is a non-profit 501(c)(3) organization that specializes in providing interpretive programs for private railroad excursions, group rail tours, and various outreach events. In a typical year, we have more than a dozen events planned throughout the Upper Midwest.

The APRHF Rail Rangers is very grateful for our partnership with the NICTD that allows us to provide on-board programs and route guides such as this. If you enjoyed having route guidebooks such as these, or learning about the landscape that we are traveling through, please express that to the marketing team at NICTD.

For more information about APRHF Rail Rangers, feel free to check out www.railrangers.org or www.southshoreline.org. We would also appreciate your "like" on our Facebook page to express your support for what we do. APRHF Rail Rangers appreciates any donations; everything you contribute is tax deductible thanks to our non-profit 501(c)(3) status. You can also become a member of the APRHF to support our work with onboard educational programs and for our venues in La Plata, Missouri.

ABOUT THE AUTHORS — ROBERT & KANDACE TABERN

Executive Director and Chicago Coordinator of the APRHF Rail Rangers program

It's no surprise that Robert developed a love for railroading – his dad grew up along the old New York Central line in Ohio and his mom was raised near the busy *Evanston Express* CTA line in suburban Chicago. As a child, Robert would take at least one long-distance Amtrak trip per year with his family. Kandace was born in Southern California and raised in Arkansas, but always lived near the rails.

Robert has been involved with doing narration on passenger rail cars for more than a decade now. For a number of years, he was a manager for Trails & Rails, an organization sponsored by the National Park Service that provides on-board commentary on various Amtrak train routes. Robert rode both the *Empire Builder* and *Southwest Chief* on a regular basis. In July 2015, Robert and Kandace teamed up with the APRHF to create the Rail Rangers program. Since then, interpretive guides with the group have provided educational programs on many private railcar excursions across the Midwest. Robert and Kandace were also instrumental in getting Rail Rangers docents on the train from Chicago to South Bend.

Robert and Kandace always manage to stay busy – and they're usually on the road traveling and exploring new sites together. Robert has been to more than 340 units of the National Park Service, while Kandace loves hiking and exploring caves. They co-own a railroad route guide business called "Outside the Rails"; you can find more information about it online at www.midwestrails.com. They currently have 11 different route guidebooks available for various Amtrak routes across the Midwest, plus a children's activity book and program.

When they're actually around – Robert and Kandace call the Chicagoland area home. Before deciding to work full-time in the travel industry, Robert spent much of his life in television and radio news, while Kandace worked most of her life as a pharmacy technician. They now enjoy hitting the road most weekends and exploring new places.

CHECK OUT OUR OTHER RAIL ROUTE GUIDES

Outside the Rails Book Order Form

☐ **CHICAGO-LA PLATA, MO**
Expanded Ed. $35 ☐
Abbreviated Ed. $10 ☐

☐ **CHICAGO-ST. PAUL, MN**
Expanded Ed. $35 ☐
Abbreviated Ed. $10 ☐

☐ **CHICAGO-ST. LOUIS, MO**
$20

☐ **CHICAGO-MILWAUKEE, WI**
$20

☐ **CHICAGO-QUINCY, IL**
$15

☐ **CHICAGO-CARBONDALE, IL**
$20

☐ **INDIANAPOLIS-CHICAGO**
$20

☐ **CHICAGO-DETROIT, MI**
$20

☐ **JUNIOR RAIL RANGERS**
(w/prize pack $15)

Get your best prices on these books on-line at WWW.MIDWESTRAILS.COM.
You may also order by mail. Send this form, along with your check (add $3.97 per book shipping fee), to: APRHF Rail Rangers, PO Box 175, La Plata, MO 63549.
A portion of sales is donated to APRHF Rail Rangers and the APRHF general fund.

SPECIAL THANKS

American Passenger Rail Heritage Foundation
Kathy Bruecker
Bob & Amy Cox
Fred Giure
Bjarne Henderson
Joe Kuczynski
Indiana Dunes National Lakeshore
Alane Morgan
Robert Neil
Northern Indiana Commuter Transportation District
John Parsons
Dave Poole
Russell John Sekeet
Rita Tabern

ISBN 978-1-365-87651-6

Outside the Rails is ©2017 Robert & Kandace Tabern, All Rights Reserved
Published in cooperation with the Northern Indiana Commuter Transportation District

Withdrawn

NOV 1 7 2025

Public Library Of
St Joe County